KILLER WEB CONTENT

CONTENT

Make the sale
Deliver the service
Build the brand

Gerry McGovern

A & C BLACK • LONDON

First published in Great Britain 2006

A & C Black Publishers Ltd
38 Soho Square, London W1D 3HB

Copyright © Gerry McGovern, 2006

British Library Cataloguing in Publication Data
A CIP record for this book is available from the British Library.

ISBN-10: 0-7136-7704-X
ISBN-13: 978-0-7136-7704-1

A & C Black uses paper produced with elemental chlorine-free pulp, harvested from managed sustainable forests.

Design by Fiona Pike, Pike Design, Winchester
Typeset by Palimpsest Book Production Ltd, Grangemouth, Stirlingshire
Printed in Spain by Graphycems

CONTENTS

ACKNOWLEDGEMENTS

This book is only possible because I have for many years had the privilege to meet thousands of people from all over the world. From Auckland, New Zealand to Abilene, Texas; from Reykjavik, Iceland, to Taipei, Taiwan, I've learned an awful lot and shared a few laughs.

I'd like to thank the following for feedback, ideas, advice, support, and inspiration: Abbe Winter, Abbo Paolo, Alexander Lawrence Brown, Barry Hagan, Brian Lamb, Belinda Foulds, Beverly Godwin, Bob Johnson, Brett King, Candi Harrison, Cheryl Blackford, Christopher Stewart, Clint Hyer, Darlene Baze, David Shaw, Derek Fromson, Eitaroh Arakawa, Ellen Wallace, Ellis Kell, Emma Yeatts, Fredrik Wackå, Geoffrey Thomas, Helmar Rudolph, Ian Balfour, Ismael Nafria Mitjans, James Bull, Janet Musick, Jared Spool, Jean-Marc Dubois, Jeff Wasserman, Jennifer Tribe, Jens Jacobsen, Jim Behrens, John Howze, Judith Snyder, Judy Gill, Julie Tipton, Karen O'Brien, Kay Ross, Keith Robinson, Kurt Kragh Sørensen, Lisa Carden, Mark Baartse, Mary Morel, Mats Johansson, Maurice Coleman, Mike Harper, Mike Riversdale, Mirona Iliescu, Natasha Vincent, Nate Dame, Nick Harrison, Nhan Chiem, Nigel Parkes, Patrice Kavanagh, Paul Corney, Peter Storandt, Rachael Stock, Ricard Giner, Robert Stark, Roy Young, Sandra Moffett, Sinead Nestor, Stan Halse, Stephan Spencer, Stewart Stephens, Tizneem Nagdee, Uwe Grunewald, William Brown.

PART ONE: THE THEORY

It may work in practice, but does it work in theory?

1 DO YOU HAVE THE KILLER INSTINCT?

A small percentage of Web content really makes a difference. It makes the sale, delivers the service, and builds the brand. This is the killer Web content. It probably represents less than 10% of content published on the Web, because – let's face it – most content just gets in the way.

Up until now, content has been a hugely undervalued asset. In the early years of the Web, the focus was on the technical. Then it shifted to visual design. Only now are people recognizing that quality content is the essence of what makes a website successful. The Web runs on content. It is its hidden asset, its gold. Yet for so long it has been treated like coal – a low-grade, low-cost commodity best published in bulk.

In a world where everyone is publishing, how is your content going to stand out?

Do you have a nose for killer Web content? Do you have a gut instinct for when content is working and when it isn't? If you do have the killer content instinct, then *Killer Web Content* will hone it to a fine point. If you haven't fully developed it, then *Killer Web Content* will help you to understand the difference between the killer and the filler.

The opportunity to create content has never been greater. We are living through a text revolution – from e-mails to mobile phone texting, from websites to blogging, the world has gone mad for words. So you'll need to be sure your skills in creating killer Web content are well honed. Because if your content isn't the killer stuff, how on earth is it going to stand out, and who on earth is going to bother reading it? I have been involved in the Web since 1994 and have always taken a content first, technology second approach. In the early years, that was a hard sell. Nobody wanted to listen. Now they do. I have never seen such interest in Web content. This is a hot subject with great career prospects and huge career potential.

WEB CONTENT FINALLY COMES OF AGE

I have talked about Web content in 35 countries and in many parts of the United States, and I've got really good news for you: interest in Web content is on the rise. Every year, I get better and bigger audiences who really care about content. They know it is a valuable asset that, if managed well, can deliver tremendous value.

Through analysis and testing, you can find out which content works and which doesn't.

As a result of years of analysis and testing, I have discovered that there is a science to content. It may not be a hard science that has rigid formulae, but there are ways to write a sentence that will get a reaction from San Francisco to Singapore, and from Reykjavik to Rome. And there are sentences that nobody will respond to in these and other places. Across cultures and markets, there are words that work and words that don't. Words that make the sale. Words that lose the sale.

I have assembled 17 different summaries that relate to the Apple iTunes music service. I have shown these summaries to over 2,000 people in 13 countries, and have asked them to quickly choose their favorite. One summary is chosen first in practically every country. In fact, 49% of people chose this particular summary. That's extraordinary. And what's equally extraordinary is that some of the summaries weren't chosen by anyone. (We'll see later what the killer and filler summaries were.)

BUT THE WEB IS FULL OF FILLER

I used to be a music journalist. In the music industry there is the concept of "filler." Basically, the average album has ten to 14 tracks. Some artists have only five to seven good tracks ready to record, so they need to write another five to seven to complete the album. Typically, these are sub-standard tracks and are known as "the filler."

The Web is full of filler content. Generally, this content has been directly transplanted from print and doesn't serve any other purpose than to give a website some bulk. In Chapter 10 we'll learn about a company that used simply to place its brochures on its websites. Sales were flat; so it decided to create quality Web content. Year-on-year results showed an increase in sales by more than 100%.

The press release – a staple of most corporate websites – is a good example of print content that gets published because it's the easy way out. Originally, press releases were not meant to be published. Instead, they were supposed to be released to the press as a story "hook"— something that might get them interested in writing a story in their publications.

Your website is your publication. You should be taking your press release ideas and turning them into compelling stories that communicate clear messages your customers care about. Simply putting press releases up is the lazy way out. Most of your customers care to read your press releases about as much as they'd care to open a bag of two-week-old fish.

Right now, Web metrics are relatively primitive. However, metrics tools are improving. Within the next five years, the Web will become a communications channel where content can truly be analyzed and identified as "killer" or "filler." Look around you and you will see that many organizations are publishing reams and reams of filler content – just to fill up space, just because that's what's always been done, just because that's the job someone's been paid to do, just because it's so much easier to churn out filler than to hone the killer stuff.

From the best websites, the filler will be weeded out slowly but surely, and the people who create it will either have to find new roles or be retrained. (In fact, this is happening today in organizations such as Microsoft.) If you create killer content, on the other hand, you will be highly valued and highly rewarded, because it is this content that will be making the sale, delivering the service, and building the brand.

THE ESSENCE OF WEBSITE SUCCESS

I was once told a fascinating story by a friend of mine who is involved in the investment banking industry. Investment bankers were looking for investors in what they were calling "third-world economies". Nobody was having much luck. Then some banker started calling them "emerging economies" and there was a phenomenal increase in investment – all because of a couple of words.

Fortune magazine had a similar experience. For years, it had been publishing a supplement on retirement options with headlines like "Better Plans for Retirement." Then someone came up with the idea of using the headline "Retire Rich." Those two words resulted in a huge jump in sales, making that issue the most successful in the company's history.

Your customers have a small set of words that summarize what they care about. Find those words, and you're half way to success.

Words matter, and I aim to prove to you that they have never mattered more than they do today. In this hectic world, we are inundated with so much stuff that we simply home in on the things we care about. And we express what we care about in a small set of words – I call these words "carewords." I could call them "keywords," but then you'd yawn and put the book down. The problem is that – like "third-world economies" – the word itself is uninspiring. Of course, the way keywords have been used hasn't helped. Many people think that they are something you quickly add to the HTML of a page and have only a loose association with the actual content. Keywords are also associated with metadata, a word so boring it deserves a health warning. So I'm going to call them "carewords" from now on.

Listen up: the secret of Web communications and marketing success is to be found in the concept of carewords. There's something in them that has explosive potential, something that gets to the essence of modern human behavior. As Web readers, we are hunter-gatherers once again – only this time, instead of scanning the horizon for prey, we scan pages for carewords. When we see these words, we click, we act. And that is what the Web is all about: tasks and actions.

What do most people care about when flying today? Low fares or free coffee? You'd probably say low fares. When people go to a search engine, are they more likely to type "low fares" or "cheap flights"? Suppose I told you that one of these careword phrases is 400 times more likely to be typed into a search engine than the other. Wouldn't it be important for you to know that if you were working as a marketer for an airline?

Killer Web Content will give you simple, robust techniques to identify the carewords of your customers. Developed over ten years of research and practical experience, these techniques eliminate the filler and let you focus on the killer Web content.

MAKE YOUR CONTENT STAND OUT IN THE CROWD

Every day, millions of people use search engines. As a marketer or communicator, it is important for you to understand their behavior when they are searching. By analyzing how our customers search, we learn a lot about what is important to them.

Focus on how people search, not on how search engines work.

What is called "search engine optimization" is becoming an important part of business. However, some of its practitioners are missing a vital point: you shouldn't focus your energies on optimizing content for each of the various search engines. That's a short-term strategy. Optimizing your content for how and why your customers search is a much more robust and long-term strategy, because, if you optimize for how people search, you are in fact also optimizing for search engines. The business model of most search engines is based on getting the right result to the right person as quickly as possible. The perfect search engine would give you one result – the exact content that you require.

If you think about how and why your customers search and create your content based on that thinking, then you help your customers.

And, if you help your customers, you help yourself. *Killer Web Content* will help you to create content that works well for people who search, and thus works well with search engines.

FOCUS ON THE TASK

Writing for the Web is not the same as writing for print. One of the key differences is that, when people use the Web, they are relentlessly task-focused. They want to do something, and they want to do it as quickly and as painlessly as possible.

My wife's sister is a Roman Catholic nun. The last time she visited us, the conversation came around to the Web. (It invariably does, when I'm steering.) She likes the Web but said that she finds it very frustrating. I was a bit surprised. I would have expected that a nun, trained in contemplation and silence, would show more patience and serenity. Not so.

She is an expert in counseling and often turns to the Web to check the latest research. She told me about how annoyed she gets when she clicks on a search result that turns out to be irrelevant. I asked her how she did her research before the Web and she threw her head back: it was very much harder before the Web.

I thought about this for quite a while, and I realized that she was merely expressing something very human – we tend to forget quickly a major inconvenience of the past and focus on a relatively minor inconvenience of the present.

Getting in a car and driving to a library would have taken far more time than clicking on a number of irrelevant results. But that's not what matters to people using the Web. The pre-Web is the distant past. It is the now, the moment, that matters. And every moment that is wasted by clicking on an irrelevant result leads to frustration.

Content-Attention Paradox

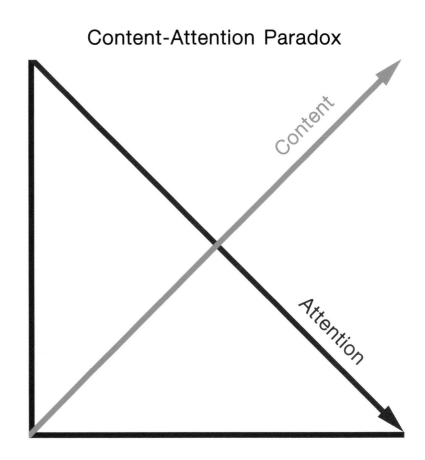

The Web is the land of attention deficit syndrome. You must deal with the content-attention paradox: you have so much to publish, yet people have so little attention to give. Attention is like an elastic band: it will stretch so much and then it will snap. People's eyes dart across pages, scanning impatiently. What's the most popular button on the browser? The "Back" button. To paraphrase Arnold Schwarzenegger, if you lose the attention of your reader because your page is badly organized and/or you've got filler content, they hit the back button, muttering: "I won't be back."

The vast majority of people come to your website to do something specific, and they want to get in and out as quickly as possible. Identifying the most important tasks that people come to your website to complete, and helping them do so as quickly and efficiently as possible, will be critical to the success of your website.

FROM GETTING ATTENTION TO GIVING ATTENTION

Someone once said that the difference between traditional marketing and Web marketing is the difference between getting attention and giving attention. I couldn't agree more.

Let's say I want to get your attention and you're on the other side of a busy road. I will probably wave and shout. Let's say I get your attention and you cross the road and come to me. What should I do now? Should I keep waving at you and shouting in your face? It probably wouldn't be a good idea.

A lot of websites are waving and shouting in their customers' faces. Big fancy intro pages, flash animations, and pop ups are all attention-getting strategies, when what's needed is to *give* some attention. Why? Because the customer has made a deliberate decision to visit us; we've *already* got their attention. Now they want to do something. They want some questions answered and they don't want anything to get in the way.

If you use attention-getting strategies on your website, you stand a strong chance of really annoying your customers.

Giving attention is about facilitating the quick and easy completion of a task. It is about having answers to the most important questions your customer has. Giving attention is what Google, Yahoo, and eBay do.

Most advertising agencies that I come across have absolutely awful websites. They're all flash and no substance, all getting attention and very little giving attention. They are so obsessed with being seen to be original that they've become ridiculous.

Take J. Walter Thompson, for example. Instead of having a "clients" section, they have a section called "name dropping." Click on that and you will find a list of clients. But it's not your usual list – no: someone photographed a business card folder. Very cool. The problem is that there are so many business cards per page it is hard to read them; so you don't actually know who some of these clients are.

Take Saatchi & Saatchi as another example. When you arrive at their website, you're presented with a big swinging logo that alternates between "Saatchi & Saatchi" and "Ideas & Ideas." There isn't a *skip intro* option, so you are forced to watch this fatuous parade for about 15 seconds. Then you are sent to a splash page where you're given two choices:

select high-speed
Click here to see how ideas can come from anywhere.

select low speed
Click here for just the facts.

These two choices say a lot about advertising thinking. If you're a poor, miserable wretch on low bandwidth, I'm afraid it'll have to be just the facts, but, if you've got broadband, well, we'll give you all these wonderful ideas. High speed = creativity. Low speed = the boring facts. Tell that to Google, the ultimate low-speed website. Isn't it funny how it has managed to build such a global brand by being low speed and functional?

The Web works best as a no-frills, functional place. A great website gets to the point. It is useful.

This is not a rant against graphics, animation, or creativity. It is very important that your website is visually pleasing. However, it is much more important that your website is *useful*. Websites that are popular and profitable are useful – they allow people to do something practical.

THE CUSTOMER IS STILL KING

So much changes; so much remains the same. As a marketer and communicator, the skills that you have been taught are absolutely relevant when it comes to the Web. As communicators, we are all taught to think of the reader. As marketers we are taught to put the customer first.

If there is one underlying problem that I have found in every one of the countries I have done Web work in, it is the difficulty organizations have in truly putting the customer first on the Web. Many organizations want to put the customer first, but organizational inertia or the daily grind of work usually shoves such noble aspirations to the side.

Genuinely putting the customer first is a winning formula on the Web. Ask Amazon or Google.

For now and for the future, the most important competitive advantage you can have is a deep understanding of what your customers care about and a relentless focus on helping your customers to fulfill their needs. *Killer Web Content* will show you simple, proven methods that will help you to put your customers first today and always.

WHO THIS BOOK IS FOR

Killer Web Content is for you if you know that merely creating content is not enough. If you believe that getting people to read your content and to act on what they have read is where the real test lies, then this book is definitely for you.

It is for professional marketers and communicators. The natural home of a public website is with marketing; the natural home of an intranet is with communications. However, *Killer Web Content* is also for IT (information technology) people who would like to focus more on the *I* in IT.

This book is for bloggers. If you've got an opinion and you want to express it on the Web, then you want to ensure that your content has the best chance of being read. Otherwise, you would be better off keeping what you have to say in a private diary. *Killer Web Content* will help your content stand out in the crowd.

It's also for middle and senior managers. Unless you intend to retire in the next five years, you cannot ignore content management. This is a critical new management discipline. Content is now an asset, a driver of sales, of service delivery, of productivity, a builder of brand. You must understand how to get the maximum value from your content for the minimum cost. *Killer Web Content* will show you how.

This book is not just about commerce – it's about websites that need to drive actions. I've done a lot of work with government websites over the years. The best government website creators realize that they too are in the business of sales and marketing and that they need to sell and market the uptake of online services. They need to convince the skeptical citizen that doing business with government is easier and faster on the Web.

The universities which are making the Web work are focusing on killer Web content. Universities are often hotbeds of politics and ego. Under the guise of academic freedom, university websites can become a tangle of different designs, overflowing with filler content.

Killer Web Content is for those running intranets, too. Some organizations take the awful view that because it's "only staff" they can afford to pile in lots of poor quality, badly organized content. The best intranets know that they can't take their staff for granted and that they need to enable them to quickly find content that will help them to do their jobs better.

I'll tell you who this book is not for. It's not for the "put-it-upper." That, unfortunately, is how so many websites – intranets in particular – are still managed. Treating content like bags of potatoes or coal doesn't work if you want to derive any value from it.

Historically, the Web has been seen as the responsibility of IT. That was understandable when the Web was new and nobody other than technical people really understood it.

The printer was the rock star of the 15th century. Yes, it was sex 'n' drugs 'n' printing. Printers – people who produced print, that is – were invited to dine with princes and kings. That's because the Gutenberg printing process had just been invented and everyone thought that printing was cool.

When the 16th century arrived, the printer was old news. The new cool was publishing, and the hip dude was now the publisher.

and has been around for a long, long time. Don't listen to the "more" gene when you're managing your website.

DON'T CONFUSE CHANGE WITH PROGRESS

I was there during the whole dot-com boom. It was an era of tremendous energy and gross excess, when ridiculous ideas went for ridiculous amounts of money. We were told that change was inherently good, that speed was God and time the Devil. If you weren't living on the edge, you were taking up too much space, and, if you didn't act quickly, you were a dinosaur. Unfortunately, some of us confused change with progress. I watched senior executives make multimillion-dollar decisions after about five minutes of analysis. Some of these decisions went horribly wrong and the executives lost their jobs. These were smart people, who were too busy working too hard and who couldn't find the time for proper analysis.

I'm sure you've been in a situation where you've been forced to make a decision without having had enough time to think it through properly. I know I certainly have, and practically every time I have made such a rushed decision I have paid dearly for it.

"Don't confuse 'novelty' with 'innovation'," wrote the acclaimed management thinker Peter Drucker. "The test of an innovation is that it creates value. A novelty only creates amusement . . . The test of an innovation – as is also the test of 'quality' – is not: 'Do we like it?' It is: 'Do customers want it and will they pay for it?'."

Equally, don't become a "Flash" addict. Not all that rotates is gold. Google is the Ferrari of the Web and Nike.com is the tractor. The last time I tried Nike.com, the navigation moved as my cursor approached it. Imagine if you were driving along a motorway and the signs moved as you approached them.

There is one word that describes all great Web brands: useful.

Every time I hear the word "branding" in a conversation about the Web, my impulse is to reach for the sick bucket. It's not that I don't think branding is important. I did a degree in marketing, and I believe that genuine branding is absolutely essential on the Web. It's just that so many people who talk about Web branding are actually thinking about Web gimmickry. Shiny toys. Eye candy. Things that get attention. Novelty.

Jeff Bezos, founder of Amazon.com, came up with the best definition of branding I have ever heard: "Branding is what people say about you when you leave the room." Successful Web brands are rugged, functional, sharp, and focused.

NO NEED FOR PANIC: ENTER THE "LESS" GENE

The "less" gene is here to help us to make the best of our lives. Much younger and often not as aggressive as the "more" gene, the "less" gene has gained substantial ground in the last 50 years.

More = Filler; Less = Killer.

You don't judge a book by its weight; you don't think a film that is three hours long is twice as good as one half the length; you don't buy your newspaper because it has twice as many stories; and you don't go to websites because they have millions of pages. Instead, you listen to the "less" gene, which helps you get by in this crowded world.

PUBLISH THE WEBSITE YOU CAN MANAGE

Most early websites were not really managed. They were at best administered. I have a technical name for Web administrators. I call them the "put-it-uppers." Filler or killer content mattered little to the put-it-uppers; they just put stuff up. There's not a great future for put-it-uppers, because putting stuff up on a website is little different from putting stuff up in a supermarket. (Website put-it-uppers get paid more – for now.)

There is a great future for take-it-downers and for it'll-never-get-up-in-the-first-placers. (We used to call these *editors*.) There is a great future for people who think about what they need to publish, and about what they don't need to publish. There is a great future for those who publish a website they can manage.

Do you overreach with your website? It's a very common problem. Partly, it's because we manage websites as projects rather than as processes. Partly, it's because we're listening to the "more" gene, which repeats in a monotone: "Have gigabytes. Must fill. Have gigabytes. Must fill."

Most websites I have had experience with start off with the view that everything is a good idea, and the cooler the idea the better. Not too long after those websites have been launched, though, it becomes apparent that nobody wants to know about updating content or bringing all the cool ideas to the point of maturity.

Ultimately you will be judged, not on the size of your website, but on the value it delivers.

Organizations love projects because projects can have a definable budget and time-frame. Getting a search engine or a staff directory for a website is a project. However, search engines and staff directories require processes if they are to be effective.

Quality search is more a process than a project. It adheres to the classic adage "garbage in, garbage out." If your content isn't written for how people search, then the quality of the search results will be greatly reduced. Your staff directory might be an application, but it runs on content. If you don't update your staff directory, then people aren't going to be able to find who they need.

Publish a website you can manage. If you only have one person to manage your website, then only have a website that one person can professionally manage. There is no point in creating a website that requires three people to manage if you only have a single resource. That resource will be stretched to the limit and you'll end up with a lousy website. Nobody will be happy – not the people who come to your website and not staff or management – because your website will not achieve its objectives.

If you – or some member of your team – has not read every single page on your website in the last 12 months, then your website is not being professionally managed.

Today, many websites are damaging the reputation of the organization. Every time someone finds the wrong content or clicks on a broken link, the brand is hurt. Out-of-date content and malfunctioning applications are major issues on the Web. This is a particular problem for large websites.

Every year the proportion of old content grows in relation to new. Much of the old content is out of date and should be removed. However, because on a lot of websites there is no process in place to review content, the out-of-date content continues to grow.

When was the last time you, or a member of your team, read over all the content on your website? Now don't tell me you're too busy.

THINKING ABOUT THE STRANGER MAKES SENSE

Deep in our heads is a small fist of a brain – the limbic region – that is a shortcut to our nerves and oldest emotions. This is the seat of instinct, impulse, and reflex actions. This "fight or flight" control has served us well for millions of years and we should not ignore it, but neither should we be a slave to it.

For five million years, our ancestors were "violent, mobile, intensely suspicious of strangers, and used to hunting and fighting in bands of close relatives," according to Paul Seabright in his fascinating book *The Company of Strangers* (Princeton University Press, 2004). Then something happened about 10,000 years ago that began a series of extraordinary and rapid changes for this "shy and murderous" species.

Some say that advances in language were a foundation for this change. Seabright believes that another reason was that humans began to trust strangers and that this led to an explosion in trade. "Most human beings now obtain a large share of the provision for their daily lives from others to whom they are not related by blood or marriage," he writes.

To organization man, the customer is an outsider, a stranger.

If I'm asked to analyze a website, one of the first things I look for is how the name of the organization is used. If I see lots sentences beginning with the organization's name, if I see lots of we-focused content, I know that this is a "primitive" website. It is the most natural

The "busy" Web work will be outsourced, whether it is Web design, programming, or writing. The work that requires serious thinking will stay in-house, because, in a knowledge economy, productive thinking is where the return on investment is. Make sure you stay on the right side by being productive, not busy.

Get yourself a "stop doing" list.

It is not productive to be too busy publishing more and more Web content to do any of it well. It's not a "to do" list you need but rather, as Jim Collins points out in *Good to Great* (HarperCollins, 2001), a "stop doing" list.

"Most of us live busy but undisciplined lives," Collins writes. "We have ever-expanding 'to do' lists, trying to build momentum by doing, doing, doing – and doing more. And it rarely works. Those who built the good-to-great companies, however, made as much use of 'stop doing' lists as 'to do' lists. They displayed a remarkable discipline to unplug all sorts of extraneous junk."

You need to give 80% of your attention to the 20% of things that really matter. Give 20% of your attention to the 80% of things that are not as important, and decide to stop doing 60% of those things. Give 0% to the multitude of things that don't matter.

If you can stop doing the things you really don't need to do, then you are on the path to discovering the core patterns that, if you focus your energy on them, will bring you success and fulfillment. While the "more" gene will always want more, more, more, you must focus on thinking smarter and working smarter, so that the result is quality from top to bottom.

MAXIMIZE THE INPUT, MINIMIZE THE OUTPUT

The economic view of the world has been based on the scarcity principle. Efficiency and productivity are focused on minimizing input and maximizing output. Traditionally, the "more" gene is what industry has been about: getting more out of less.

Much concerning the information economy is counter-intuitive. It is about maximizing the effort of input so as to minimize the quantity of output. Much more film ends up on the cutting room floor than in the final version. Fewer words will appear in the final report than were originally written. (At least, fewer words *should* appear!) Unfortunately, the traditional IT industry has often focused on maximizing output. That, however, is changing.

Peter Drucker wrote that we've spent the last 50 years focusing on the *T* in IT – the technology. He believed we'll spend the next 50 focusing on the *I* – information. When it comes to content, technology can help, but whether you create killer or filler is up to you. Technology can make it easy for you to set up your own blog, but it's you who has to write it. Put it this way: would Shakespeare have been a better writer if he'd had a word processor?

For years, I have seen organizations invest substantial amounts of money in content management software without having any content management *strategy*. It was as if they expected to set this software running and then wait for it to start churning out high quality copy. For a while, it was all about distributing publishing capability as widely as possible within the organization. Fine in theory, but what happens when you distribute publishing capability to people who can't write? Think about it.

YOUR JOB IS TO DRIVE ACTION

Knowledge is what you know. It's the useful stuff inside your head; it's what makes you valuable. The most valuable knowledge is the most difficult to automate or outsource.

Information is the communication of knowledge. It should be treated as a verb, not a noun. There are two key ways to measure the value of information:

1. **It must deliver new knowledge. The people you are informing must know something they didn't know before they read your website.**

2. **Those people must be more willing to act as a result of the knowledge they have received. This is a critical factor in this age of relentless noise. Your information succeeds when you drive the action you intended to drive.**

Content is the formal expression of information – it is information written down, photographed, recorded, or somehow formally structured. Content needs to drive action, and if it doesn't, it's not delivering value.

The challenge you face is that the consumer you are trying to get to act as a consequence of reading your content is being asked to act by lots of other websites too. Why should they read you? Why should they act in response to your content?

THE EMERGENCE OF THE ORGANIZATION OF ONE

It's not just your customers you need to focus on with your content; it's also your boss, your potential boss, your peers, and those who report to you. (Do people read and act on your e-mails or do they simply delete them?) You will be managing information and, increasingly, you will be managing yourself. This is an age in which we need to brand ourselves, an age in which professionals have become – to a lesser or greater degree – an organization of one.

That's really what the blogging phenomenon is about – the expression by millions of individuals of their personal opinions. A blog is saying, "Please read me. I have something to say." The blog is the calling card of the organization of one, and its core message is often, "I'm very smart. Give me a job."

The move is on from the organization man to the organization of one.

The traditional organization is not going to be there for you quite like it was back in the day of the organization man. You're on your own more now. You may end up working from home some of the time and will have to supervise yourself. You will have to resist that extra coffee break or that walk with the dog when a deadline looms. Equally, you will have to resist overworking yourself, as the curse of many who work for themselves is that they do nothing but work. So don't let the freedom to be your own boss mean that you end up becoming your own slave.

If a tree falls in the forest and nobody hears it fall, did it really make a sound? If you do something and do not communicate what you did, did you really do it? In this age everything of true value gets done twice. The first time is when you actually do the task; the second is when you get it down as content – you might post something on your blog or you might write up a more formal report for the intranet. One way or another, you need to make sure that your smartest moves are published. In academia they say "publish or perish." Well, on the Web, it's publish or perish too.

TESTING, TESTING, TESTING

If successful retail is all about location, location, location, then successful content management is all about testing, testing, testing. Increasingly, information economies will focus on ways to measure the value of the information they publish. Very little work has been done on this crucial area, and most organizations hardly have a coherent information strategy, let alone a way to measure the effectiveness of particular pieces of content. However, we are going to see major changes over the coming years in accounting practices and management theory.

Microsoft, for example, is moving towards a publishing model in which the impact of its content is measured. Microsoft used to have a big bang publishing model. When a new version of Microsoft Windows or Office was to be released, a huge writing project was initiated to write about every aspect of that product. Writers sweated as the deadline loomed, the test being whether the content would ship in time with the product.

This resulted in a quantity-driven publishing approach. Whether the content worked or not was not the issue; it was about writing something on everything and getting it out through the door on time. The Web began to change things because for the first time the impact of content could actually be tested. In one environment, Microsoft found that out of almost 6,000 documents, 50 were receiving 19% of visits. In other words, 1% of the content was receiving 20% of the readership.

The Web has allowed Microsoft to move to a continuous publishing model. Instead of working hard writing lots of content, Microsoft writers are working smart, identifying the areas that need content and spending time writing well about them. Writers are now getting feedback on whether their copy is actually working for the readers. (Is it helping them to complete the tasks they wish to complete?) Get good feedback and your star will rise in Microsoft; get poor feedback and you'll be facing a rewrite.

We already have wonderful tools that tell us the value of the physical things in our factories and offices. The Web is the first medium that allows us to comprehensively measure the value our content creates.

The ultimate test of content is in the actions that it drives – in the end, you will be measured by and rewarded for the actions that you deliver with your content.

Content is the hidden asset in many organizations, and to grow and continue to be profitable – and to keep a competitive edge – organizations will need to tap into this asset in a way they never have done before. The better organizations are going to focus increasingly on what content is working and what is not.

Test, test, test. Finding killer Web content requires testing, testing, testing.

You must find ways to discover how people respond to your content. Here are some things you should consider:

- **Make sure you have accurate, consistent data about your website. Many Web managers have extremely poor data coming through on website activity. To be blunt: if you can't measure it, you can't manage it. Make it a number one priority to clean up your data.**
- **Focus on action points on your website. How many people are visiting the home page and then leaving? How many people are failing to fill in forms? How many new subscribers to your newsletter did you get this month? How many repeat visitors did you have this month, as against once only visitors?**
- **Test, test, test. The data will only tell you so much. The best Web managers make it part of their daily routine to interact with their customers. As a manager, there is no greater skill you can develop than to have a deep understanding of how your**

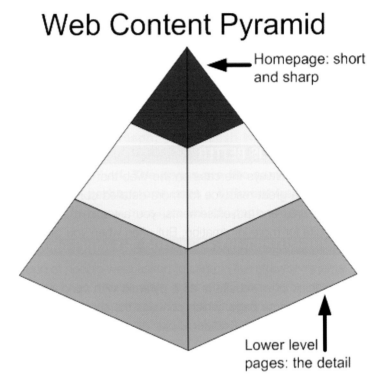

Web Content Pyramid

Homepage: short and sharp

Lower level pages: the detail

I wanted to book a holiday home for my family. I went to lots of websites but most of them had only a single picture of the holiday homes. It wasn't enough. I was prepared to pay good money and I wanted a much better sense of what the holiday home looked like; I wanted more pictures.

When it comes to content, a compelling, clear message should come before conciseness. If more copy will make the message clearer and more compelling, then we need more copy. We can structure our websites so that the detail is kept at lower levels, thus allowing people to read it if they so choose. Nevertheless, the general rule of "less is more" should be your guide.

There's a bit of the put-it-upper inside all of us, a bit of the "more" gene striving to get out. In fact, I have rarely come across 1,000 words that can't be edited down to 500 and made clearer and more compelling.

TOO MUCH JAM IS BAD FOR YOU

In his book *The Paradox of Choice* (Ecco, 2004), Barry Schwartz writes about another jam study in which a group of people was given the opportunity to sample a selection of high-quality jams. In one instance, there were six jams available to sample; in another, there were 24.

Choosing from six jams

Choosing from 24 jams

The smaller sample of jams attracted fewer people. However, 30% of those people went on to buy some jam. Of those who had the opportunity to sample 24 jams, 3% made a purchase.

This is classic "more" gene behavior – more is initially attracted by volume and can't resist the opportunity to check all the jams. Then the "more" *gene* shuts down, overloaded by so much choice. The "less" *gene* focuses on the six jams, tastes, and makes a decision. For the shop selling the jam, less is unquestionably more.

Choice takes time. It also takes thinking, and too much thinking can lead to stress and indecision. As we are exposed to ever more external stimuli, we have less and less attention to give to any one thing, and so we begin to ignore.

Look at it this way: suppose it takes a minute to taste and decide to buy a jar of jam, and 30 seconds to taste and decide not to buy. We have six jams and decide to buy one. That's one minute for the jam we buy, plus 2½ minutes for the jams we don't buy – a total of 3½ minutes.

If, however, there were 24 jams and we bought one of them, the total time taken would be 12½ minutes – one minute to decide on the jam we want, plus 11½ for the jams we decide not to buy. That's a lot of time and a lot of deciding, and most of us couldn't be bothered.

Our taste buds would be overloaded so, by the time we'd have tasted the seventh jam, we'd probably have forgotten the taste of the first jam. And if we decided not to taste some of the jams, we might wonder whether we were missing something.

At a certain point, the more choice we have, the more hassle it becomes. The elastic band of our attention snaps. So we avoid the process and buy the blackberry, because that was our favorite jam as a child and we simply don't have time for all this choice.

The more people are bombarded with choices, the more they begin to react from the gut, doing the thing they've always done. For you to succeed, you must be able to think from the gut of your customer – not your own. You must be able to use the carewords your customers use. You must temper your gut instinct so that you can better understand the gut instincts of others. You must maximize the input by selecting from a wide range of jams, and minimize the output by presenting the very best jams to your customer.

That's not an easy task. But then, if it was easy, you'd outsource it.

3 WHY CONTENT IS *NOT* KING

Until the Web arrived, most organizations didn't value content. Even now in a typical organization, the higher up you go, the less appreciation there is. That's all beginning to change because content has become a hidden asset of great value.

In the early years of the Web, content still took a back seat. On a typical Web project, if the writer got paid X, then the graphic designer got paid 2X, whoever did some basic programming and HTML got 3X, and, if there was advanced programming involved, then that person got 4X. In other words, the writer was the worst paid by far.

I was telling someone who runs a Web agency about this, and they agreed. In fact, they never tell a client that they are giving them a writer because they know that the rate will drop through the floor. They come up with some fancy name instead, something that sounds a bit technical.

Here's how a typical Web project used to work: IT spent lots of money on some content management software, which it then handed over to marketing, who in turn got a graphic design company to create some concepts. Half way through the project, someone mentioned that content would be needed for the website before it could be launched. The manager in charge of the project got the most junior person they could find to round up some content from the other departments. If this content was absolutely awful, the manager might get this junior person to rewrite it. Or perhaps they had a summer intern who could throw a few words together. That's how content was treated in many organizations.

MODERN MANAGERS WRITE AND READ A LOT

A friend of mine has a senior position in one of the world's largest and most prestigious organizations. This organization is relentlessly profit-focused and pursues excellence in practically everything it does – with the exception of content.

My friend gets about 100 e-mails every day from other staff in the organization. He ignores about 85 of them. The 15 or so e-mails he doesn't ignore often have attachments or significant points that need to be addressed. At least half of his day is spent dealing with these e-mails.

What an incredible waste! This is a big organization with thousands of people. If each employee is ignoring 85% of the e-mail from other employees, then this is an extraordinary – hidden – productivity drain. This performance-obsessed organization is being amazingly sloppy.

I have another friend who works with a big software company. He told me that he had done some basic calculations and that, by his estimation, the company spends more on publishing content about its software (marketing materials, support documentation, etc.) than it does on writing the code that *creates its software*!

The management of content is now a cornerstone of good management.

A few years ago, I stood in front of an MBA class and showed them a slide of a computer. I asked how many had one of these. Every hand went up. Then I asked them to imagine that we were transported back twenty or thirty years. "If I posed the same question," I asked them, "do you think I would get the same response?"

Old style managers didn't use computers – they had secretaries to do that sort of typing work. Old style managers managed by walking and talking, meeting and greeting, wining and dining. Generally, the role of reading and writing was a minor one. That has all changed; today, managers spend an increasing proportion of their day reading and writing e-mails and instant messages, reading and preparing reports and presentations, and reading and writing content for intranets and public websites.

Managers, and the organizations they work for, are simply not properly prepared for the explosion of content that has occurred since the early 1990s. Content management will become a cornerstone of good management in this century.

ARE YOU READY FOR THE CONTENT BOOM?

It's a really good thing for content that these older managers are moving slowly towards retirement and that younger managers are getting into more senior positions. Many older managers have, I believe, a hidden prejudice against content. In their minds, content reminds them of the menial task of typing. To them, content is not real work, and it is certainly not an asset.

Just underneath them, though, the "text generation" is rising. The digital revolution has been – so far, at least – a revolution of words. The written word was in decline for most of the latter half of the twentieth century. Radio, film, and television grew in popularity, and, as cheap color print production was introduced, the image began to dominate in much of the print medium. And there is absolutely nothing wrong with that. The visual image has been a dominant part of human communication for millions of years. In the grand scheme of things, it's only relatively recently that that the written word has risen in importance.

The Internet has ushered in a new text revolution. Search, e-mail, websites, cell-phone texting, and blogs, are all text-based activities.

So text matters. Content is the new oil. The Web content industry is at pretty much the same point as the oil industry was in the 1930s: the beginning of a big, long boom. Are you ready?

The explosion in the quantity of text-based content has far outstripped content management thinking and capabilities. Over the coming years, we will tap into this hidden asset. It's going to be a slow change, but then slow change can be the best change of all.

The Web has changed how we communicate. Because communication is core to who we are, changes in it tend to have a profound impact and thus take time to digest. So don't get frustrated. Proper content management requires a long-term view of things.

YOU CAN IMPROVE HOW YOU THINK

Don't get caught up in all the noise that surrounds the now. You must take time out to think – great writers are first and foremost great thinkers. You've got to keep asking yourself where you want to be in five years' time.

You can't have great content if you don't have great thinking.

Content is really thinking that has been written down. You can't have good content if you don't have good thinking. Thinking involves asking questions such as:

- **What is the task?**
- **Who is it for?**
- **Do they actually care?**
- **What is the best way to write about it?**
- **What can I learn from the last time I did it?**

Intelligence is a gift. Thinking is the skill with which we use that gift – and that skill can be improved.

You can improve your thinking by first understanding that thinking is not the same as intelligence. According to Edward de Bono, a pioneering writer on thinking, "intelligence is a potential. Thinking is a skill with which we use that potential." While intelligence is more akin to a natural gift, thinking is a skill you can improve if you're prepared to work on it.

Being very intelligent doesn't necessarily result in great thinking. "In my experience, highly intelligent people are not always good thinkers," de Bono writes. Of course, intelligence matters. Combine great thinking with great intelligence and that's a recipe for genius. But sometimes, intelligent people don't feel they need to train to think – they assume they're above that.

Learning how to think is not the same as learning what to think; there's a world of difference. You should always be hungry to learn about new ways to improve your thinking. And you should always be wary about buying prepackaged ideas.

ALWAYS MAKE TIME TO THINK

Killer content requires quality thinking, and quality thinking requires quality time. Don't ever allow yourself the excuse that you're too busy to think. Anyone who is always too busy to think has no future worth talking about.

When it comes to learning to think smarter, be realistic, disciplined, and set limits. A lot of people fail because they expect – even want

— to fail. You don't train for a marathon by running 20 miles the first day. So, don't start off your blog by writing 15 posts on the first day, only to write nothing new for the next three weeks.

Thinking is not something done well in bulk; it's hard to sit down every Monday for four hours and do all your thinking for the week. Instead, there should be a thinking process going on in your head most of the time. Your mind must always be ready to question if you come across something that is interesting or problematic.

However, you *do* need to take some time when you're doing nothing else but thinking. I'm sure you've had weeks that went by in a blur. You were so busy you didn't have time to think. As we have already established, being busy is not the same as being productive, and, if you are so busy you can't think properly, it is highly unlikely you are being as productive as you could be.

Every day, find some time when you do nothing else but think. Start off with five minutes when you are at your sharpest. Five minutes of quality thinking is plenty to begin with, and resist when that "more" *gene* urges you to carry on. Be disciplined and gradually build up your thinking time, but never overdo it. Thinking for longer than 30 minutes at a stretch is very tiring and probably unproductive. The important thing is that you think every day, with maybe a break at the weekends. Set a time limit for this quality thinking time. If you are addressing a particular problem, say things like: "I'm going to think intensively about this for five minutes." Setting limits creates focus and a sense of discipline.

Think slowly.

"Think slowly and try to make things as simple as possible," de Bono writes. Think slowly? That's an interesting concept. Don't smart people think really fast? If you're lucky, you might find one big idea during your lifetime. You've got time.

GET YOUR IDEAS DOWN

Ideas aren't much good unless they are translated into action. Your mind is a wonderful place, but it can be a little lazy. So, if you have an idea you think is interesting, write it down immediately, because getting it written down – no matter how rough the draft – is a vital step towards turning it into killer Web content.

Putting your ideas down on paper moves them a step closer to reality. Leave them for a couple of days – or preferably a couple of weeks – then give them a critical review. Most you will dismiss but, now and then, one idea will stand out.

Many of the world's greatest geniuses didn't depend on their memories; they knew about the lazy mind. Beethoven was quoted as saying, "If I don't write it down immediately I forget it right away." Picasso and Einstein were never without their notebooks.

It's not just artists who wrote things down. Alfred Sloan (who built General Motors) once said: "If I do not sit down immediately after the meeting and think through what exactly it was all about, and then put it down in writing, I will have forgotten it within 24 hours."

IF THE CUSTOMER IS KING . . .

Thinking is crucial, and so is content, but on the Web actions speak loudest. Websites need to be able to improve productivity, increase profitability, and deliver better services. Content is just a means to these ends, and your real focus, therefore, must be on the customer, not the content.

Content is not king for the very same reason that the product is not king. The maxim that tells us "The customer is king" clearly emphasizes that we should focus first and foremost on the customer. Likewise, then, the reader – not the content – is king on the Web.

We now move from the theory of killer Web content to the practice. The chapters following examine everything from how to identify your reader, through how to create killer content and be a great blogger, to how to optimize your content for searching. However, we'll start off by getting to know the reader/customer better.

PART TWO: THE PRACTICE

Know your reader

I'd like to introduce you to Mary and her daughter, Jennifer. Jennifer has been having a lot of teething problems lately – at least that's what the doctor says they are. Mary is not so sure. She has two other children and they didn't cry the way Jennifer does.

I'd also like to introduce you to Tomas, a young and ambitious doctor. Tomas graduated five years ago and belongs to a group of general practice doctors in an affluent and fast-growing town. I know it's just a quick introduction, but a little later we'll get a chance to know Tomas, Mary, and Jennifer better.

4 WHY YOU NEED TO BAN "USERS"

Every time I hear the world "user" I shudder a little. I find it one of the ugliest words in the English language. It's dehumanizing. It strips people of personality and humanity. It's a generic, meaningless word. Calling people "users" is the same as calling them "winkniks" – it carries as much meaning, and has as much warmth and humanity.

Bicycle users? Horse users? Car users?

If you saw someone on a bicycle what would you call them? A "cyclist," probably. Hardly a "bicycle user." Why do we call people on bikes "cyclists"? Because cycling is the dominant activity and, when people are using tools, we generally give them names based on the dominant activity. Now, we could say that people on bikes are "handle-bar holders," or we could say that Lance Armstrong is one of the world's greatest "saddle-sitters," but we don't, any more than we would call someone in a car a "car user" or someone on a horse a "horse user."

"User," you see, is so general that it is meaningless. We use everything. To call people users gives us no sense of focus on what the dominant activity is, or what we need to do to help the person to complete that activity well.

What is the dominant activity on the Web? It is reading. Sure, people read differently on the Web. They scan-read – they're highly impatient – but the dominant activity is still reading, whether they are using a search engine, filling in a form, buying a product, or getting support. If you understand and focus on how people read, you are on the right road to designing an effective website. So, call people "readers" and it will help to clarify exactly why they are on your website. (There is another good reason. Drugs and the Web have some unfortunate common vocabulary: "users," "traffic," and "hits.")

When you no longer use the word "users" and instead have "readers," "customers," "mothers," "teenagers," "businessmen," then – and only then – can you create killer Web content.

Of course, calling someone a reader is only an intermediate step. We need to become more specific. By calling people readers we are forced to ask some important questions:

- **What is it is they care about reading?**
- **Do we have what they want to read?**

We need to do something that is incredibly difficult: we need to put ourselves in the shoes of our most important readers.

DO YOU MAKE THE MISTAKE EVERYBODY MAKES?

There is one mistake people make that pretty much ensures they will not be able to create killer Web content. It is one of the most common mistakes in all writing – and practically everybody who writes has been made aware of it at some stage – and it is this: writing for the ego, not the reader; writing from the organization's perspective, not the customer's. You know about this mistake, as you've heard about it many times before. Yet no matter how obvious it is, it's the single biggest thing that destroys killer content.

It is incredibly hard to write for the reader and not for the ego. It means going against millions of years of human behavior, where survival meant looking out for ourselves and the small group we were associated with. It is still more natural for us to think primarily about ourselves and the organization to which we belong.

To write killer Web content, you must accept three things:

1. **Driven by millions of years of conditioning, your customers focus on their own needs and those of their family and loved ones.**

2. **Making your customers feel special means understanding what they really care about.**

3. **What they really care about can sometimes be the opposite of what you really care about.**

Many of the world's best-known writers have gone to great lengths to understand their readers. John Steinbeck created an imaginary, idealized reader, while Stephen King pesters his wife to read his drafts.

The first and most vital step in creating killer Web content is to create a small set of living, breathing readers. People you can think of as you write. People you have empathy for and can care about. People you want to design the best website in the world for. "Persona" is now a popular term for these people, so I'll refer to them as "reader personas" from now on.

LEARN THE EDITOR'S GREATEST SKILL

If you are the editor of a local newspaper in Longford, Ireland, you will have a deep understanding of what the people of Longford really care about and want to read about. You will have developed your understanding through years of interaction with these people. You will go to the football matches, pubs, church, fairs, and other places where Longford people gather. You will be where the people are, because that is how you keep your finger on the pulse of public opinion.

Let's say that a magazine called *Seventeen Rocks* is looking for a new editor. Two people apply for the job. One is 21 years old and the other is a bed-ridden 77 year old. Who do you think has the best chance of getting hired?

There are a lot of 77 year olds running websites today. They live in cocoons, in perfect isolation. Many of them have hardly even met their readers, let alone had a conversation or ongoing relationship with them. Occasionally, they will commission a survey, and they might even look at some website logs. However, they don't *know* their readers, and if you made them the editor of a local newspaper in Longford, the paper would fold in six months.

If you are in charge of a website – an editor, in other words – you must interact with your reader on a daily – or at least a weekly – basis. It must excite you to talk to and observe people and find out what they truly care about, because that often involves listening for what they *don't* say.

Some of the things your readers really like, you might not like at all.

Your Web team depends on you for one thing more than any other: to tell them what readers really care about. To do this, you must have developed a fine gut instinct and your finger must always be on the pulse. If you've done this, then you will be able to listen to an idea and immediately sense whether it's a runner or not. You will choose an idea, not because you like it, but because you know your readers will like it.

I want you to imagine you are the managing editor of the website of a large pharmaceutical company called Lagver. Lagver launched its first public website in the mid-1990s. Its website was for doctors like Tomas, whom we met at the beginning of this chapter. That's because that's who this pharmaceutical company traditionally sold to.

Some years after the launch, the company decided to do some market research. It was shocked by the results. Only about 7% of the people coming to its website were doctors. However, 60% of visitors were categorized as "patients and caregivers."

The people you target offline are not necessarily the people you need to target online.

After more research, Lagver found that there was a dominant segment within the patient and caregiver group. Think of a family. If there is someone sick in a family, who is most likely to go on the

Web to research the illness? The mother – someone like Mary, say, whom we also met at the beginning of this chapter.

That's a big change, isn't it? From writing for doctors to writing for mothers. The problem was that many of the Lagver staff responsible for writing content for the website would rather this research had never been done. They were comfortable writing for doctors; in fact, a number of them were doctors!

Writing for mothers like Mary required a significant mindset shift at Lagver. Doctors might have been comfortable with a term like "cardiovascular disease." However, mothers preferred a plain-English expression like "heart disease."

It's not just mothers who prefer plain English. According to Overture, a leading seller of Web advertising, 8,863 people searched for *cardiovascular disease* in May 2005, while 196,173 searched for *heart disease* – 22 times more people used the latter phrase. While 176 people searched for *cardiovascular disease symptom*, 6,635 searched for *heart disease symptom* – 38 times more. (Overture is a free service. Wordtracker.com, a paid service, is more powerful and accurate.)

Not until the Web have writers and editors had the opportunity to find out the words that really matter to people. On the Web, people think in and search using carewords. Writing with your readers' carewords, as I will examine later, does not simply make your content more likely to be found, it also ensures that your customers will feel more comfortable and at home with your content, thus increasing the likelihood that they will act.

WHAT DOES MARY WANT?

Even when presented with the results of the research, most of the writers for Lagver subconsciously think they are writing for Tomas, because in him they see themselves. Tomas is a medical professional like these writers and editors, and they really want to tell him how great a medical organization Lagver is.

Getting the writers to think about, focus on, and write for Mary and other mothers like her is going to be an extremely difficult task. We're talking about a culture change here. This company is not used to writing for mothers, patients, and caregivers.

Some within Lagver might legitimately make the point that, just because there are lots of mothers like Mary coming to the website, it doesn't necessarily mean that the website should have content for them. Lagver, after all, cannot sell directly to mothers. However, while Lagver does indeed sell its drugs and other treatments directly to doctors and pharmacists, it knows that the Web has changed the medical landscape. Before the Web, patients were much less likely to question their doctors or have opinions on the types of medicines that they considered suitable for their needs. Now, many patients do research on the Web and then suggest things to their doctors. People like Mary are using the Web to become much more educated and informed.

So Lagver decides that it is important to have content for people like Mary on its website. What sort of content? Let's say Mary wants to find out more about babies' health. She might type the carewords "baby health" into a search engine. Suppose she gets a set of results that includes links to the following websites:

- **Her country's department of health**
- **A major health insurance company**
- **A professional journal on children's health**
- **Lagver**

Which link is she likely to click on? I have asked this question all over the world and I have hardly ever found anyone who felt that Mary would click on the link to the Lagver website. Trust is a cornerstone of publishing. Once you have identified your reader, one of the first questions that you need to ask is whether they will trust your content.

You must know what content your readers will trust you with.

If I was an editor of the Lagver website, I would need quickly to establish what content Mary would trust me to supply her with and what not. Perhaps Mary won't see me as a trusted resource for general health information, but she will see me as a source of information on my company's products? These are fundamental questions, and the only way I can even begin to answer them is by having a deep understanding of Mary and caregivers like her.

KEEP THE NUMBER OF READERS SMALL

The most important benefit of creating fictional people like Mary and Jennifer is that you externalize the target of the writing process. Mary makes you stop thinking about your needs and the needs of your organization and helps you to think about what she cares about.

By putting faces on Mary, Jennifer, and Tomas, you change your reader from an invisible user into a real human being with real needs. If you are a good writer and editor, you will have empathy with Mary and understand that she is naturally worried about the health of her beautiful baby. That's why she's at your website.

Your readers need to become an integral part of your day-to-day work. You may develop an initial outline of them based on extensive market research and discussion, but they cannot live just in some report. An effective Web manager/editor will carry their readers around in their head, constantly thinking about their needs. That way, every time they hear a content idea, one of the first questions they will ask themselves will be, "Would Mary find this useful?"

Your reader needs to stand beside you as you write.

You should aim to have three or fewer reader personas (with a maximum of five). If you have more than five, you and your team will find it hard to remember their names, let alone have a deep understanding of how they feel and think. You want to create readers that you can care about – or, at least, understand – because, if you care about them, there is a greater chance that you will know what they care about.

Choosing three well-selected reader personas will almost definitely be sufficient to meet the 80-20 rule. From the human cell to the Web, networks tend to obey this rule. It is also known as the Pareto Principle because it was originally formulated by Italian economist Vilfredo Pareto, who stated that wealth distribution followed a predictable law, with a small percentage of people accumulating most of the wealth.

If you are like the vast majority of organizations – and I include governments, universities, and other non-profits here – then the 80-20 rule dictates that a small number of reader personas will help you to achieve most of your objectives.

It is a fallacy that you can reach everybody on the Web. Try to reach everybody and you will certainly reach nobody.

There is a view that the very strength of the Web is that it is a "world-wide" phenomenon and that you can indeed reach everybody and answer every question that anybody might have to ask. This is a dangerous myth. Besides the fact that designing and managing such a website would be hugely expensive and complex, such a website will simply overload your reader. Remember that when someone comes to your website you are charging them their time and their attention. If it takes too long for them to find what they need, and/or if you lose their attention because you have given them too many choices, they will hit that most popular of buttons on the browser: the "Back" button.

DEALING WITH CONFLICT BETWEEN YOUR READERS

Johan is an ambitious young man with a bit of cash on his hands. He's not in the super-rich category. He's doing okay and doesn't want to leave his money lying in the bank getting a miserable return. Johan is just the type of investor that Lagver wants to target.

Currently, Lagver's investor base is nearly all large institutions, and the board would like to spread it more. The investor relations manager has done some research that indicates that the Web could be a perfect vehicle to do this. The research indicates that large institutional investors don't come to the Web so much, as they have brokers to supply them with the advice they need. However, for individual investors who like to do their own research, the Web is perfect.

For you, as an editor of the Lagver website, knowing this is very important when preparing content for the Investor Relations section. So you might include a case study about someone just like Johan who invested a sum within his financial range five years ago, and show the return he has received.

There's a bit of a problem, though. The needs of Johan and Mary are not the same – in fact, to some degree they are conflicting. Let's say Lagver had record profits in its previous trading year. What sort of heading are you going to have on the home page?

Record profits – but we still care!

Unless you're very lucky, your website will have readers with conflicting needs and outlooks on life. Getting the style and tone just right requires real skill, and the only way you're going to be able to do this is to know your readers inside out.

THE LEVEL OF DETAIL YOU NEED FOR YOUR READERS

You don't need to get into huge detail about the personal lives of your reader personas. Mary, as a mother, sees herself as responsible for the health of her family. What type of movie Mary likes is not that relevant. Johan is an ambitious young professional who has some spare cash. It doesn't matter what sort of suits he buys or whether he prefers latte to espresso coffee.

So, what does your reader type need to have?

- **A name**
- **A face**
- **A place – where they live**
- **A little history**
- **Three or fewer major tasks that they come to the website to complete**

RELENTLESSLY FOCUS ON THE TASK

The Web works best as a self-service environment, and self-service design needs to be convenient and fast. Other design challenges may require an understanding of the goals people have. However, Web management requires a relentless focus on the task.

The Web is a brutal landscape, full of impatient scan-readers and competitors who are just a click away. The people who matter come rushing to your website to do something specific. That's why you must focus on the most important task of the most important reader first. Everything else will have to wait.

Please resist the desire to satisfy everyone in your organization by polluting your home page and website with every piece of content you have. That is a guaranteed recipe for disaster, and it is you who will ultimately be held to account.

Welcome to Aer Lingus,
Ireland's national airline.

in our website you'll find travel details, flight schedules and information on Aer Lingus – everything you need to make your travel plans.

Failte

They say a picture paints a thousand words. Well, what does this picture paint for us?

Hi, we're Aer Lingus, an airline, and we've got planes! Not just one plane; as you can see from our lovely picture, we've got at least three. And, of course, we've got pilots – because you can't fly a plane without a pilot, can you? Not to mention our beautiful, smiling in-flight attendants.

We've been sitting around wondering just what our customers might be considering when they think about flying to Ireland. And then we came up with that killer piece of content: "Welcome to Aer Lingus, Ireland's national airline." Because we all know that every day of the week countless people go to search engines and type in "Ireland's national airline." So now you know! We hope you enjoy our site.

With this website, Aer Lingus nearly went bust. You could partly blame 9/11, but, really, Aer Lingus had taken on many of the worst traits of an entrenched monopoly. Then the market changed, and Aer Lingus had to compete with ultra-competitive, cheap-flight airlines like Ryanair.

Aer Lingus had one last chance and it took it with both hands. It went through a radical transformation, bringing in a young, aggressive senior management team and shedding many employees and costs. This resulted in a much leaner operation and much lower prices. Here's the type of home page the new Aer Lingus came up with.

I have shown this page to thousands of Web professionals in many countries. The immediate reaction of many is to shudder and draw back. When I ask how many people think it is an ugly page, as many as half of the audience will put their hands up.

A great website will tell you its killer tasks the second you look at it.

This home page saved Aer Lingus. It changed it from an airline on the verge of bankruptcy to an airline that, in 2004, delivered the highest profit in its history and was the second most profitable airline per passenger in Europe after Ryanair. In 2001, Aer Lingus was doing 3% of its bookings online. In 2005, it was heading towards 70% – a phenomenal achievement by any standard.

The new Aer Lingus home page may not win any graphic design awards but, as far as marketing strategy goes, it is hugely successful.

There are three core target customers for this page:

1. The Irish traveler

2. The American traveler

3. The British/European traveler

However, there is one overriding message that is impossible to miss:

Book a cheap flight now!

The Irish traveler represents the major share of Aer Lingus business, and so gets the lion's share of the home page. The United States is a very important market for Ireland, and so there are clear offers for American travelers. This focus, of course, relates well to that of the Irish tourism industry overall, where the Irish, Americans, and British represent the largest portion of the market. Let's have a look at three reader personas of the Aer Lingus market.

Peter and Joan McBride

- **Irish**
- **Middle class**
- **Two-week holiday and occasional weekend if they can find a bargain**
- **Very family-focused**
- **Want amenities for kids**
- **Interested in self-catering**
- **Will eat out**

Tom and Elizabeth O'Neill

- **Irish-American**
- **First visit**

- **Want to check out their roots**
- **Saved for years for this trip**
- **Bargain hunters**
- **Love the countryside**
- **Want to hire a car**
- **Tom – fishing, golf**
- **Elizabeth – traditional music, theatre**

Suzy and friends
- **British**
- **Fun-loving**
- **Love Dublin**
- **Want a mad weekend**
- **Parties are a must**
- **Sleeping is a chore**
- **Just want a good time!**

So, what we hope is that Tom and Elizabeth don't end up in the same hotel as Suzy and friends, because they won't get a wink of sleep. Knowing about Peter, Joan, Tom, Elizabeth, and Suzy and friends is important if you are running a tourism website offering accommodation and vacation packages. However, does it really matter to Aer Lingus what all these people want to do when they arrive in Ireland?

The people who really matter to you are task driven and time starved. Keep it simple: relentlessly focus on the task.

Aer Lingus have gone for a brutally simple approach. They assume that everyone who flies to Ireland wants to book the cheapest flight possible in the shortest time possible. Therefore, the home page screams:

CHEAP FLIGHTS!

You don't have time to get into niceties on a homepage. You need to hit your readers straight between the eyes with your best killer Web content. They're scanning, hovering above the page. You need to let them know why they should land.

On the Web, it's all about the task, the task, the task. If you go to eBay.com, for example, you will likely see three big words running across the top of the page:

1 Find   *2 Buy*   *3 Pay*

The rule on the Web is: know your readers and know their key tasks. Have only content that helps them to complete these tasks. Everything else just gets in the way. Focus relentlessly until you discover the find-buy-pay of your website, and then make sure that people can start finding, buying, and paying the second they arrive.

IMPATIENT

Nobody wants to wait; nobody wants to spend a second longer reading than they absolutely have to. Usability expert, John Rhodes, talks about an ad used in the New York City subway system in the 1980s that read

If U Cn Rd Ths, U Cn Mk Bg Mny

I don't think there are too many of the Web and text-messaging generation who would have any problem reading this ad.

The mind is wonderful but it has limits. There's only so much we can or want to take in at any point in time. Therefore, as the quantity of information around us increases, the percentage that we exclude increases. What we take in becomes even more compressed as we bring meaning down to its bare essentials.

The eye looks at a sentence, identifies the most important words – carewords – and then the mind makes lots of assumptions. That's why it is so hard to proofread your own work; you see what you thought you wrote rather than what you actually wrote.

What our eyes see is

If U Cn Rd Ths, U Cn Mk Bg Mny

What our mind understands is

If you can read this, you can make big money

"Most people just look at the first couple of words – and only read on if they are engaged by those words," according to *Eyetrack III*, a fascinating 2004 study of how people read on the Web. All my years' experience on the Web validates this finding. (I have also found that search engines give more emphasis to the content near the top of a page and near the beginning of a sentence, but I'll look at this in greater detail in Chapter 9.)

Your customer will scan the heading and, if that's interesting, they'll scan the beginning of the first sentence of the first paragraph and, if that's not interesting, they might start reading the second sentence. However, what is more likely is that they will skip to the first sentence of the next paragraph, or perhaps hit the "Back" button. The eye doesn't read so much in a flow but rather in a series of jumps, of stops and starts.

When reading, people zero in on the top of a page and the first half of the first sentence.

The following diagram shows where the eye pays most attention on a typical webpage. Priority 1 (red) is where the eye looks first on the home page. Priority 2 (yellow) is the next most popular space, and Priority 3 (green) gets the least attention. Clearly, from this *Eyetrack* study, the top left of the page, followed by the centre, is where the eye focuses most on a webpage.

Priority 1   Priority 2   Priority 3

TYPICAL EYE BEHAVIOR ON A WEBPAGE

People are highly skeptical on the Web. There is so much material being thrown at them, they don't know what to believe. So much content is inaccurate or out of date that the natural impulse is to become conservative and rely on only a small set of trusted websites.

People also don't particularly like reading from a screen because it's harder than reading from a page. It also tends to be less comfortable, as it's much easier to curl up in bed with a book than a notebook. All of these factors mean that it is not easy to write killer Web content. Whether writing for your website or your blog, Web writing is probably one of the most difficult tasks you will face. That's why you need to be armed with the six "Cs" when you sit down to write:

1. Who Cares?

2. Is it Compelling?

3. Is it Clear?

4. Is it Complete?

5. Is it Concise?

6. Is it Correct?

WHO CARES?

Care is a soft word but a hard question. Who cares? We know that Mary cares about the health of her daughter, Jennifer, and that of the rest of her family. We know that the typical air traveler cares about a cheap flight. I know that my children care a lot about having cool ring tones for their mobile phones. What does your customer care about?

People are too overloaded with information today to waste time on things they don't care about. It's about time: your time and their time. "Invest your valuable time only where you will get a return," states Marshall Goldsmith, considered a world authority in helping successful leaders achieve positive change in behavior. "The time that you are wasting in attempting to coach people who don't care is time that is stolen from helping the people who do."

Don't fall into the trap of assuming that, just because you passionately care about something, your customer will. This is one of the biggest mistakes you can make. Sometimes what you care about can stop you seeing what your customers care about.

Ban the use of the following statement: They might be interested in reading this.

This is a dreary statement and will lead to a dreary website full of filler content. Every time there is a suggestion for new content, ask the following question three times: Who cares?

BE COMPELLING

Simply knowing what people care about is not enough. You need to sell. You need to make people pay attention. You need to be compelling.

That's why the *Fortune* magazine heading "Retire Rich" is so powerful: it is a compelling, concise, and clear statement of what people really care about. I have given audiences the background on this heading, and then asked them to guess it. People have often come up with the suggestion "Retire Early." Nice idea. However, there's little point in retiring early if you're retiring poor.

Being compelling has much to do with identifying and using the carewords that matter to your customers, and I'm going to focus specifically on that in the next chapter.

BE CLEAR

If your content is not clear, you will lose a huge percentage of people almost immediately. Many talk about simplicity in writing but few practice it. To make things simple is not to make them simplistic. In a complex world, you must communicate complex information in a simple and clear manner. Albert Einstein talked about the real challenge being to make things as simple as possible and no simpler.

People are constantly coming down escalators on your website; they are scanning for the trains, tickets, and toilets. You might want to sell them souvenirs but first and foremost they want to know where the toilets are. Make sure your toilets are well signposted, clean, and properly functioning before focusing your energies on anything else.

One of the keys to creating an effective website is to make sure the basics are done well, but I often find that Web design teams get bored with doing the basics and want to do some exciting, innovative, cool things. Resist that urge. Remember, you get paid to be bored. An innovation must be truly useful, otherwise it's just eye candy.

The better you know your subject matter, the more difficult it is to write clearly about it.

You are the worst enemy of clarity on your website because you know your subject matter so well. That's why you must always stand with your audience and think from the perspective of Mary or Johan. Clarity requires empathy and an unrelenting focus on the needs and the level of understanding of those you are writing for.

Whatever you do, don't show off – you don't need to tell the reader you are intelligent by using the biggest words you can find; you don't need to tell them that you studied French by throwing in a French quote; and you certainly don't need to get in a reference to that book you read last month that really impressed you: this is all generally filler.

Filler includes your pet phrases, so track them down and eliminate them. Whenever you write something you are impressed with – something you think the reader will be very impressed with – be extremely wary.

When we talk, we are interacting with other people, and there are all sorts of signals that we watch out for. Our words are given greater emphasis by our tone and pitch. Our bodies talk too, and those we interact with can ask questions or show other crucial signs of understanding or lack thereof.

Content is not like that. It doesn't have all those informal aids to meaning and it doesn't get that essential feedback; so it must be a lot clearer than speech, and much better thought through.

Read your writing out loud and watch out for even the slightest stumble, smallest sign of confusion, or the sections that make your ego swell. Pounce on all these signs; strip the content down to its bare essentials. Because – guaranteed – any lack of clarity you find in the content will be multiplied at least tenfold by the reader.

COMPLETE THE TASK

What is the task you wish your customer to complete? You must figure out the actions you want to drive with your content. The essence of a Web link is to help people to complete a task. Links are connections between content, allowing people to move from one step in the task to the next.

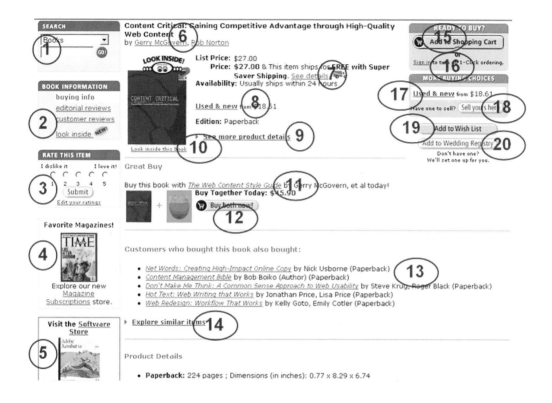

This is an amazing webpage, and it's not just because it's about my previous book, *Content Critical*. It's also because it's an Amazon.com webpage, and nobody does e-commerce better than Amazon.com. This page sure knows how to sell books. Practically every question you might have in helping you to decide whether to buy or not to buy is answered – or has a link to an answer – on this single page.

Let's look at how Amazon does it.

1. If you're on the wrong page, Amazon lets you quickly search again.

2. You can get quick links to editorial and customer

reviews of the book you're interested in, and look at sample pages from the book.

3. You can rate the book – a classic word-of-mouth technique.

4. You are told about other products on offer. This is a major challenge, particularly for large websites, because people are so task-focused they rarely see anything that is not related to the task.

5. Again, you are told about other products.

6. You can find out more about the authors.

7. You can find out more about Super Saver Shipping.

8. If you think the book is too expensive, you can perhaps buy a used copy. (A book like *Content Critical*, of course, could never be too expensive.)

9. You can see more product details.

10. You can look at sample pages from the book.

11. If you buy this and another book, you get an extra discount. This is classic selling. You walk into a store thinking of spending $100 and because you met such a friendly sales person you walk out having spent $300, feeling happy – at least until your credit card statement arrives.

12. The "Buy both now!" button is that extra call to action.

13. More classic word-of-mouth selling with the "Customers who bought this book also bought" feature.

14. You're encouraged to "Explore similar items" that the customers who bought this book also bought. Amazon.com gives you an initial list of five so as not to overload you. It's your decision whether you'd like to see more.

15. You can add this book to your shopping cart whenever you're ready.

16. You can sign in for "1-Click ordering," Not 5-click or even 2-click – just 1-Click. The Web is about self-service, and self-service means convenience, speed, and discounting, and Amazon.com does it all.

17. You have another chance to check out used copies of the book. Many successful websites have key links repeated numerous times on a page. That's because people tend to zero in on a certain section of a page, with their mind blanking out the rest.

18. If, for some strange reason, you didn't like *Content Critical* you can sell your old copy. So you're not just a buyer, you're also a potential seller.

19. "Please don't go just yet," the webpage says. "If you're not sure you want to buy the book now, why not add it to your 'wish list'?"

20. "Add to Wedding Registry" – after intensive research, Amazon.com has discovered that before you get married you should read a book on content

management. (It's so you can properly classify the gifts you get.)

When it comes to selling books, Amazon.com knows how to complete the task and close the sale better than anyone. On every page of your website, you should ask these questions:

- **What is the core task?**
- **How does this page help my customer to complete that task?**

HOW TO WRITE GREAT LINKS

There are two fundamental differences between Web content and print content. The first is that people can search for Web content using their own words (and I'll examine the implications of search in Chapter 9). The second key difference is linking. If you focus on the quality of your links, you are much more likely to create killer Web content.

The link is the most important thing you will write on your webpage.

Write your links as if you are writing a heading. (See Chapter 7 for best practice in writing Web headings.) Avoid using expressions like "click here" or "download" in the text of the link. One of the links on the Amazon.com page is "Edit your ratings." This is a quality link in that it clearly tells you what the objective of the link is. This link doesn't need to say "click here" in the same way that a door handle doesn't need a sign beside it saying "hold and push down, then pull."

Place links at action points in your text. A link is a call to action. You should aim to have relatively short text with clear calls to action at the end. Avoid placing links within the body of the text, particularly near the beginning of a sentence. Remember, the link is saying "click on me because the rest of this text is boring."

The following example is from an Irish government website. I needed to renew my driver's license and I ended up at this page. Luckily, I had learned government speak and knew that a D.401 was a driving license renewal form. So, imagine you wanted to renew your driving license and you came to this text, what would you do?

How to apply

» Download and complete application form D.401 (pdf). This form is used to apply for, or renew a driving license. **Please check with your local Motor Tax Office that they accept applications on downloaded application forms**. Alternatively, you can obtain this form, from your local Motor Taxation Office, or you can request a copy of form D.401 by post through Oasis. Your completed

If you were like me, you would have clicked on the link "Download and complete application form D.401 (pdf)." I did this, filled it in, mailed it. Sometime later, I retraced my steps because, well, that's the sort of thing I do.

It was only then that I read the statement: "Please check with your local Motor Tax Office that they accept applications on downloaded application forms." Let's ignore the fact that this statement is totally contrary to practically everything a good self-service website is about (convenience and speed); it totally misunderstands how people read on the Web. We scan-read at speed for the right link and then we click. If you want someone to read important content first, make sure you place the link *after* the content, not before.

BE CONCISE: IT'S NOT A MURDER MYSTERY

Your website is not a murder mystery, so tell them who did it in the heading and the very first paragraph. Nobody is going to wait until the last paragraph to discover the essence of what you're trying to communicate. Lead with the need. Get to the point. Then stop.

Microsoft writes some of the best – and not so best – content on the Web. For me, the killer Web content for Microsoft is its security updates. I like the type of update webpage shown below – Windows Security Updates Summary for December 2004. The thing I like most about this one is the nice link in the centre of the page stating: "Skip the details and go to Windows Update now."

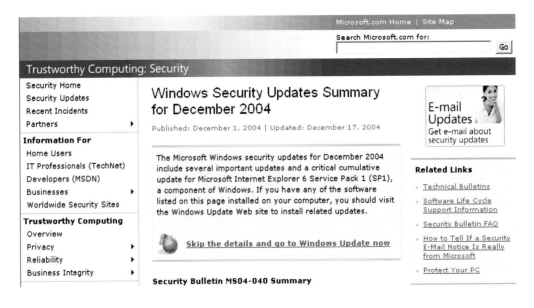

My experience of Windows Update is that it does all the compatibility checking for me, and I obviously need the update, because otherwise I wouldn't be at this page. I don't need the background – the details – I just want to start downloading the update.

Hide the details. If in doubt, cut it out.

I don't like arriving at the type of webpage that follows – September 2004 Security Update for JPEG Processing (GDI+). There's a lot of detail here that I really don't want to read. It goes on and on, and then, further down the page, gives me lots of link options. I just want one link, however. Hide the detail, I'll read it later (I promise).

The most natural tendency in the world is to overwrite. You wonder whether someone has really got the point, so you want to hammer it home. There's nothing wrong with a bit of repetition, but there's a thin line between it and filler – be careful not to cross it. When it comes to clarity, if in doubt, spell it out. When it comes to conciseness, if in doubt, cut it out.

One of the best ways to write concisely is to start off by setting a word limit. If you expect content to get read today, you need to keep it very short. For a typical writing exercise, I use the following rule of thumb.

100 words	You've lost 25% of your readers
300 words	You've lost 40%
500 words	You've lost 60%
1,000 words	You've lost 80%

Now it may be that what you really want is the last 20% – that they're the people who will buy – and, if that's so, then fine. It is important to understand that being compelling, clear, and complete should always come before being concise. If you need to spend more time on a subject to be clear, do that.

However, I have found that many people – including myself – have a habit of overwriting. Setting a word limit is certainly one of the most important techniques I have developed over the years.

Reading is a bit like mountain climbing. The longer you read, the more tired you get. A lot of people find 300 words more than enough, while I think most of us hit a wall at 500. At 1,000 words, you're talking about altitude sickness and coffee deprivation. People need a break, and only the very hardy are going to get to 1,500 words and beyond.

The vast majority of customer satisfaction surveys can be boiled down to just one killer question. According to "The One Number You Need," an article in the *Harvard Business Review*, this question is:

"How likely is it that you could recommend [X] to a friend or colleague?"

BE CORRECT

In a cut-and-paste world, it's easy to pull together some content. You might read something in a newspaper, hear it on the radio, or come across it on the Web. It's an interesting quote and it confirms what you've been thinking, but that doesn't mean it's correct.

Checking facts is hard, boring, and unsexy work, and that's why on many websites it doesn't get done well – if at all. It's much easier to quote a "fact" than to verify it. Being loose with your facts may well work in the short term, but remember that the digital world has a very long memory. So much is being recorded today as e-mail, on the Web, on video, or in audio. More importantly, so much of what is recorded is more accessible. Never before have so many people had access to what you've written. In years to come, something you said in a rush might come back to haunt you.

Editing is quality control for writing. Without editing, you're going to get things wrong. And if you keep getting things wrong, you will damage your reputation. Writing is rarely easy, but it can sometimes feel as though you are getting into a flow as the words stream out onto the page. Editing, on the other hand, is about getting out of the flow, because our minds often fool us into "seeing" what we think we wrote on the page but not what we actually wrote; that's why it's not a good idea to self-edit.

Hire a professional editor on an annual basis to review your writing. It will be one of the best investments you will make.

If at all possible, get someone else – preferably a professional editor – to look over your content. It may not be possible to do this on a regular basis, but I highly recommend that you have a professional editor review a sample of your work at least once a year.

If you have to self-edit, here are some tips.

1. **Take your time. There is a certain rush to just writing, writing, writing. Quality content doesn't work that way. You should allocate up to 40% of the overall writing process to editing. Otherwise, you're going to have filler, not killer.**

2. **Never edit immediately after writing. If possible, leave the first draft for a week. If not, leave it for a day. At an absolute minimum, get up and have a coffee or go for a walk.**

3. **Aim for a minimum of three passes. The first is about ensuring the content is compelling, clear, and complete. The next is about making it concise and correct (sometimes called copy-editing). The final edit is about proofing the corrections you made. I often edit ten to 15 times and still miss mistakes. One test I use is that it's not ready until I read over it and have no compelling reason to change anything.**

4. **Here's a copy-editing trick: use a ruler and read backwards through your text, one sentence at a time. (No, it's not satanic, though it could be useful to have a box of headache tablets nearby.) By reading backwards, you force the words and punctuation to stand out more.**

5. **Copy-edit tables, text in pictures, quotes, headings, and so on separately. Often what we do when copy-editing is focus our attention on the main text. We**

then miss that line of text underneath the picture or that heading above the table.

6. Do a word count every time. We need discipline. If it's 500 words, then it's 500 words – no excuses. Don't listen to the "more" gene, imploring you to write a couple of hundred words more.

7. Avoid throwing away your first draft; instead, cut it in half. The first draft is often a painful process, and the urge is strong to throw it away and start anew. The temptation is to start afresh, because re-reading stuff can seem very boring in prospect. There are nearly always good ideas in a first draft, so work with them.

8. Change the environment. It is extremely difficult to do a thorough edit on any content without printing it out. Read it out loud, change the font size, use double spacing, etc. Break the pattern of seeing what you thought you wrote.

9. Role-play: pretend you received it from someone else. Pretend it's from your worst enemy and you're going to show them how good content should be written.

10. Avoid major changes near the end of the editing process. A quality piece of content develops a sense of wholeness and completeness. If you make a major change in the second to last paragraph, it will have all sorts of subtle – and not so subtle – effects on the rest of the text.

11. Set a deadline and stick to it. There comes a point when it's as good as it's going to get, and you have to let go.

BEWARE OF "SMELLY" CONTENT

Can you stand by every single piece of content on your website? Can you swear that it is all accurate and up to date? When was the last time all of your Web content – and I mean *all* – was professionally reviewed?

One of the most common and damaging problems I come across is out-of-date Web content. If quality content is a hidden asset of the organization, then out-of-date content is a disaster waiting to happen.

The Web is not the same as print. Content stays around until you make a deliberate decision to remove it. What is written in a newspaper or magazine will soon fade away. What is published on the Web remains and is always a search or a click away.

In my 2001 book, *Content Critical*, I asked the reader to imagine they were booking into a plush hotel. There's a basket of fresh fruit on the reception desk. It's a nice touch and you take an apple.

A couple of weeks later, you arrive at another hotel late at night. It's raining, you're tired, and the next hotel is 50 miles away. You walk through the door and are hit by an incredibly nauseating smell. You struggle to the desk and are greeted by a receptionist wearing a gas mask. You're getting dizzy now, so you place your elbows on the desk to steady yourself.

Slowly your eyes are dragged to the bottom of the desk, where a big bowl of rotting, stinking fruit lies. It's got fungus. It's got ooze, a river of it, flowing over the edge of the bowl and down the desk. It is sticking to the elbow of your new suit.

You begin to fall backwards in a faint. "Why would anyone leave a bowl of rotting fruit on a desk?" a voice inside your head asks. "It must have been left there for months." But just before you hit the ground, you think about your website and all the rotting, stinking content that's there.

Get rid of your rotting content or it will come back to haunt you.

Wouldn't it be wonderful if content smelled? It's Friday evening, and, instead of removing that out-of-date content, you decide to go out for a drink with friends. Monday morning comes along, and, fresh and ready for work, you boot up your computer. What a pong! You have to hold your nose as you search out and delete that out-of-date document.

We would never leave rotting fruit on a reception desk, yet we leave masses of putrefaction on our websites. It may not smell but it sure does stink, and it is damaging your reputation and your brand. The credibility of your content is vital because, if the impatient, skeptical scan-reader gets the slightest sense that the content is not accurate or up to date, they will hit the "Back" button.

6 CAREWORDS: THE KEYS TO ACTION

When you discover the carewords of your customers, you discover what makes them click. Words drive actions on the Web. There might be many thousand words published on your website but there are only a very small number that really matter to your customers. Even in the most complex environments, there are core patterns and common tasks. Carewords are the core patterns of your website. They help people simply and quickly complete common tasks.

Carewords make up the core patterns of content.

Networks, in particular, have core patterns (and the Web is a network). Take river networks, for example. "Scarcely anything can look less planned and lacking in design than the drainage basin of the Mississippi," Mark Buchanan writes in his book *Small World* (Orion, 2003). "Nevertheless, this random, haphazard appearance disguises a hidden order. If every river network is unique, they are also in many respects deeply similar, indeed, even identical."

"The way to trace the outlines of the process behind river network formation is to work backward," Buchanan writes, "first by ignoring almost all the factors that might conceivably affect the evolution of a river network and starting with a few of the most obviously important."

When scientists followed this approach, they discovered that the Nile, the Amazon, the Mississippi, the Volga – in fact, every river network they studied – had the same core pattern.

Carewords are the core patterns of content. There is a best way to write headings, summaries, and paragraphs, and in each case identifying the carewords of the customer you are writing for is the first essential step.

If carewords are the core patterns of content, then self-service is the core pattern of the Web itself, and understanding the essential principles of self-service will help you to understand how to make the best of the Web. There are three core principles of self-service:

1. Convenience

2. Speed

3. Price

People are cheap on the Web. Partly, that's because of the early history of the Web, where so much was free. However, it's also due to the fact that, when you're doing something for yourself, you expect a discount.

When you go to McDonald's, you don't expect to pay as much as when you go to a plush restaurant. In a plush restaurant, you pay to wait. You also pay for the service so you expect to get it. When it's self-service, you're servicing yourself. You're taking on work the vendor would otherwise have to do; so that perennial question arises in your head: What's in it for me? Go to the home pages of Amazon, eBay, Priceline, or Travelocity – they've all got special offers.

"This doesn't apply to me," a lot of people tell me when I advise them to have a cheap website. They tell me that they run a university, non-profit, government, or other website where people don't expect you to be cheap. What are the top government-related terms people

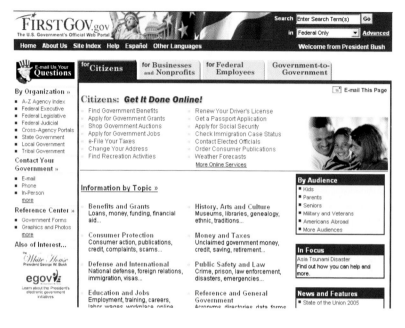

search for? Benefits and grants. The U.S. FirstGov website understands this, that's why the first two links under "Get It Done Online" near the top of the page are:

1. Find Government Benefits

2. Apply for Government Grants

The first classification in the centre of the page is

Benefits and Grants: Loans, money, funding, financial aid

A government does two basic things to citizens: it takes money from them in the form of taxes, and it gives things back in the form of services. Nobody wants to pay tax, and FirstGov has the sense to know this. FirstGov leads with content that makes the citizen feel good that government is working for them – benefits and grants.

Maybe you can't be cheap. However, there's no way of getting away from being convenient and fast. Convenience is critical to the success of self-service. It must be easy. If a self-service environment requires too much learning, the impulse is always to do it the way you're used to doing it.

You absolutely must be fast. You don't pay to wait in McDonald's. And you don't pay to wait on the Web – that's why people hate those Flash intro webpages; that's why they always click "Skip Intro."

That's why people love Google. Look at the simplicity of the Google home page, the entire weight (images and HTML) of which is less than 15 KB. Google is the Ferrari of the Web. It downloads and drives like a racing car because it knows that nobody wants to spend a second longer searching than they absolutely have to.

CAREWORDS COME FROM THE GUT

It's not so much that people are overloaded today; it's more that they are offloading the things they don't think are important. Here lies a major irony of the age of mass communication: the more communication people are exposed to, the more they are shutting off and depending on their gut instinct.

As a marketer and communicator, this means that you will need to constantly manage – and perhaps retrain – your gut instinct so that you can have an absolute focus on the gut instinct of your customers.

Web self-service creates a greater distance between the customer and the organization – a distance that needs to be bridged.

The drive towards self-service reflected in the Web is just one more trend that signals a distancing between the organization and the customer. Staff are expensive and technology is cheap; so the more you can get technology to do, the greater the profits you will make.

However, as organizations automate more and more of their processes, they isolate themselves increasingly from their customers. As "touch points" between the organization and the public are closed down, there is a need to develop new ones. Otherwise, the organization becomes out of touch – not a good idea in a fast-changing world. (Blogs can be a good idea because they keep you in touch with your audience, as we'll see in Chapter 8.)

A McDonald's manager told me that she was in her office one day when head office called. The first question she was asked was what she was doing in the office: if you're a McDonald's manager, you're supposed to spend most of your time in the restaurant. Self-service is very hard to manage and design for from a distance. You need to be up close and observing.

Wal-Mart is another master of the self-service model. It has also embraced technology more than most companies. However, it has never lost sight of the need for a deep understanding of the customer. The more it has focused on self-service, the more Wal-Mart has realized that its management must – as its primary duty – be out with its customers.

"I never viewed computers as anything other than a necessary overhead. A computer is not – and will never be – a substitute for getting out in your stores and learning what's going on," Sam Walton, founder of Wal-Mart, wrote in *Made In America*. "In other words, a computer can tell you down to the last dime what you've sold. But it can never tell you how much you could have sold . . . That's why we at Wal-Mart are just absolute fanatics about our managers and buyers getting off their chairs here in Bentonville and getting out into those stores."

There is no more valuable skill than the ability to thoroughly know your reader.

Great editors are also on the road, on the floor, on the phone, in the pub, or wherever they need to be to get the story. Chatting with David Shaw, the editor of scottish-enterprise.com, he told me about how he had previously been the editor of a highly successful Scottish fishing business magazine. Four days of the week he was on the road, out at the ports, talking to fishermen, getting to know exactly what was important to them.

I asked David how many days he was out on the road now that he was editor of the Scottish Enterprise site. None, was his answer.

It's a strange thing that technology can shut us off, make us feel that we don't need to get our hands dirty any more in the round of human interaction. But the opposite is true. If you want to manage a successful self-service website you must invest a significant percentage of your time interacting with and observing your readers. This is an absolutely critical point. If you take no other idea from this book, please take this one: getting out among your readers is by far the most important thing you can do if you want to identify killer Web content.

In self-service mode, people go on gut instinct.

When people are in self-service mode, they're rarely fully conscious of what they are doing. They act on gut instinct, and good self-service design is so simple even an adult can understand it, but designing something that simple is very hard work. Asking people directly what they want from your website is rarely a good idea. They will be unable to tell you because they follow their instinct. So you need to be able to observe and read between the lines of what people say to you. All great editors have a bloodhound's nose to sniff out what people *really* want.

I remember seeing the report on a test of a couple of hundred people whose online shopping habits were being analyzed over a two-month period. Before the test, they were given a questionnaire, and one of the questions related to how often they checked the privacy policy on a website they were buying something from.

About 40% said that they would regularly check the privacy policy. However, after the two-month period, the data was analyzed and it was found that less than 5% regularly checked the privacy policy. So, what people tell you they do on your website may not be what they actually do.

However, in other tests it was apparent that, while people rarely click on a privacy policy link, they like to know it's there – when it's not, they get agitated. So "privacy policy" may still be a careword phrase, even if one that has only subtle implications.

FOLLOW THE CAREWORD TRAIL

On the Web, we hunt for the content we need to complete our tasks. The last time I wanted to buy a laptop computer, I started my search with two carewords in my head: *laptop*, *notebook*.

I scanned webpages as a hunter would scan the horizon, and if I didn't see those carewords I got impatient.

When I found a link for laptops on a page, I clicked on it straight away. Now the trail was warming up and a new set of carewords came into play. I didn't want to see every laptop available; that was way too many.

I travel a lot, so my next set of carewords included *ultra-portable, ultra-light, laptops for traveling users*. When I didn't see these carewords, I got frustrated; when I did see them, I clicked.

As I was closing in on my prey, a new set of carewords opened up. What were they? Well, what do you think someone who travels a lot really wants in a laptop? Price? No. Memory? No. The carewords I had now were *weight*, *battery*. I wanted to buy a laptop that was as light as possible. I knew I'd have to pay a premium because cheaper laptops are generally quite heavy, so whatever I might save on price, I'd end up paying to a chiropractor (I'm speaking from experience here). And, as I frequently get stuck in airports and airplanes, I needed a good battery. It wasn't that I didn't want good performance and lots of memory, but rather that weight and battery life came first for me.

The careword trail

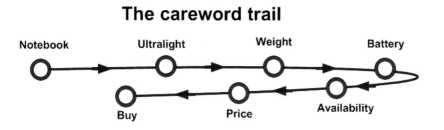

LOW FARES OR CHEAP FLIGHTS

Let's say you are thinking of flying somewhere. What might be your carewords? *Low fare? Cheap flight?* Research indicates that 400 times more people search using the words "cheap flights" than "low fares". So, if you are selling economy fares, it is important that you use the term "cheap flights" in your marketing and advertising campaign. I remember telling this to a senior executive from a major airline. He shrugged, replying that there was no way his airline would use the words "cheap flights" on its website. "It would hurt the brand," he told me. (Very sensitive things, these brands.) At the time of our conversation, this airline was in financial difficulties. No wonder. It had failed to recognize a key economic trend: customers' carewords now drive communication.

It takes time to stop thinking organization language and start thinking customer language. Successful cheap-flight airlines like Aer Lingus and Ryanair are recognizing that, on the Web, the customer controls the language.

Ryanair: The Low Fares Airline   **PREVIOUS**
Ryanair: Fly Cheaper   **NOW**

14. **Travel bookings**

15. **About us**

The above carewords define the common tasks for the Great Irish Holidays website. (There are, of course, some similar/duplicate carewords in the above list, and I will examine how we deal with these later on in the chapter.) These carewords tell us what the tourist requires.

- **They want a place to sleep.**

- **They want special offers/deals.**

- **They'd like the option of a package where everything is looked after for them.**

- **They want a "Best of Ireland" list, and a list of interesting things to do and see.**

- **They want to know about Great Irish Holidays and whether it is a company they can trust.**

- **They want to be able to contact Great Irish Holidays easily.**

The implications of these carewords are substantial. It takes a specific type of company and a lot of work to put together special offers/deals and packages, for example. These carewords are highly strategic. Should they be adopted by Great Irish Holidays, they will come to represent – in the smallest number of words – exactly what the company does.

YOUR CUSTOMERS' CAREWORDS ARE NOT YOURS

Again and again, I have found that the carewords of the organization are not those of the customer. Take Irish tourism for example. Most tourists see Ireland as a single destination. However, the Irish tourism industry sees Ireland in a very localized way. A hotel owner is only interested in promoting his hotel in his local area, for example.

The case is similar with bodies set up to promote Irish tourism. There is some attempt to promote Ireland as a single destination, but there are many bodies – both official and voluntary – that focus on promoting their particular geographic area or interests. Here are just some of the official bodies responsible for Irish tourism: Tourism Ireland, Fáilte Ireland, Northern Ireland Tourist Board, Shannon Region Tourism, Dublin Tourism, Ireland West Tourism, and South East Tourism. To some extent at least, each of these bodies sees itself in competition with the others.

Part of the tourism careword set for Great Irish Holidays included a list of geographical names. The following table shows how these names scored compared with the top 15 carewords that people chose.

Customer Carewords	Score	Tourism Body Carewords	Score
Accommodation	2,479	Dublin	263
Special offers	2,373	Regions	160
Planning a trip	1,375	Southeast	26
About Ireland	1,234	West	22
Getting here and around	1,146	Northwest	15
Things to do and see	1,084	Northern Ireland	10
Deals	1,052	32 Counties	8
What to see and do	1,032	Midlands East	0
Book travel	977	Shannon	0
Home	885	Southwest	0
Irish vacation packages	829		
Best of Ireland	793		
Contact us	741		
Travel bookings	707		
About us	557		

From the 1,000 people in 11 different countries who chose tourism carewords, hardly anyone voted for geographical words. Only "Dublin" received a significant score of 263 (out of 30,612 votes cast), but this pales in comparison with the most popular careword – "accommodation" – which received 2,479. This is not to say that geography is irrelevant to the tourist. However, when they come to a tourism home page, other things – such as accommodation, special offers, packages, etc. – are obviously more important.

Irish tourism websites tend to stress regions first. This is a perfectly natural thing to do – if you're a tourism official working in the southeast of Ireland, you get paid by South East Tourism. It's hard to grasp that you ultimately get paid by the tourists, and, if you don't serve their needs, they are less likely to visit. So, by emphasizing its organizational structure on the Web, rather than what the tourist wants, Irish tourism is creating a big problem for itself – one that is relevant to most organizations.

Some time ago, I did a careword exercise with a government department of education. I asked the staff to select what they thought were the most important carewords that should appear on the home page of the department's website. Their choices were to be influenced by the target readers they had identified, who were parents and teachers. Here's what they came up with:

1. Public consultations

2. Reports and publications

3. News and information

4. Schools

5. Policy

We then went out and asked teachers and parents to do the same. Here's what teachers chose as their top five:

1. Teachers

2. Curriculum, syllabus, and teaching guides

3. Subjects

4. Teacher lesson plans

5. Curriculum

Here's what parents chose:

1. Curriculum, syllabus, and teaching guides

2. Supporting my child

3. Exams general information

4. Protecting my child

5. School search

While there is some correlation between the carewords of teachers and parents, there is no correlation between what department staff thought should be on the homepage of the website, and what their two core target markets would like to see. Civil servants care about things like "policy" and "reports and publications," while teachers care about "teachers" and "teacher lesson plans," and parents care about "supporting" and "protecting" their children.

So please, please don't fall into the trap of thinking that what you care about as an organization is what your customer cares about. Think of Mary, Jennifer, Tomas, and Johan every day. Get your reader personas totally integrated into your work practices so that you will be speaking their language, not yours.

THE McGOVERN CAREWORD FINDER

The McGovern Careword Finder helps you to quickly identify your customers' carewords. It's a simple three-step process:

1. Prepare a list of potential carewords.

2. Get people to choose their favorite carewords from the list.

3. Analyze the results.

STEP 1: PREPARE A LIST OF POTENTIAL CAREWORDS

The important thing here is to get as wide and comprehensive a list of potential carewords as possible. Open up a spreadsheet and start listing words and phrases. Don't worry about words that are very similar; there's a method for dealing with those that I'll explain later.

Here are some places where you can look for potential carewords.

1. **Objectives: Analyze the goals and objectives of your website. For example, let's say that Great Irish Holidays – our imaginary tourism website – wants to become known as the number one website for Irish accommodation bookings. List carewords that flow from these objectives in your spreadsheet.**

2. **Ask the customer: Brainstorm with some potential visitors to Ireland to see what their carewords are.**

3. **Talk to sales reps, marketing people, industry experts, and other interested parties. Get potential carewords from them.**

4. **Do search analysis. If you already have a website and have a search engine, identify the words that are most commonly searched for on your website. Also, use services such as Wordtracker, Overture, and Google AdWords to see how people are searching on the Web itself.**

A	AG	AH	AI	AJ	AK	AL	AM	AN	AO	AP
1 Classification	32	33	34	35	36	37	38	39	Total	
2 Accommodation	49	69	117	60	81	95	58	94	2479	8%
3 Special Offers	63	59	103	63	83	64	68	90	2373	8%
4 Planning a Trip	0	31	37	53	36	17	28	21	1375	4%
5 About Ireland	47	45	36	59	48	30	58	52	1234	4%
6 Getting Here & Around	27	28	94	36	34	31	55	61	1146	4%
7 Things to Do & See	36	32	69	24	31	16	42	33	1084	4%
8 Deals	18	20	10	19	29	12	12	15	1052	3%
9 What to See & Do	24	24	26	52	38	25	28	62	1032	3%
10 Book Travel	17	17	33	12	21	0	8	38	977	3%
11 Home	24	26	0	55	15	38	23	11	885	3%
12 Irish Vacation Packages	9	24	30	8	16	7	2	14	829	3%
13 Best of Ireland	16	17	12	21	12	28	50	21	793	3%
14 Contact Us	16	11	18	33	15	40	17	6	741	2%
15 Travel Bookings	45	31	26	24	38	36	36	12	707	2%
16 About Us	2	24	26	46	11	14	27	3	557	2%

Here follows an explanation of how the table is laid out.

- Column A lists carewords, ranked in descending order from the highest score.
- Columns AG to AN show a sample of the scores given in the individual workshops. For example, in column AN, we can see that "accommodation" received a total score of 94 from the participants in that particular workshop.
- Column AO shows the total overall score for each careword.
- Column AP is the percentage each careword received. For example, "accommodation" received 8% of all the votes.

MANAGING DUPLICATE/SIMILAR CAREWORDS

From the initial results, it's obvious that there are some duplicate/similar carewords that we need to manage. For example, we have "things to do and see" receiving a score of 1,084 and "what to see and do" receiving 1,032. While it may be okay for us to alternate use of these careword phrases in the text on our Web pages, if we want to use them as part of the classification of the website, we must choose one of them.

If we did decide to amalgamate these two categories, we would also combine the scores. So now, "things to do and see" has a score of 2,116, moving it from seventh to third in the list.

WOULD YOU CHOOSE SPECIAL OFFERS OR DEALS?

The case with "special offers" and "deals" is not quite as clear-cut. "special offers" gets a score of 2,373, while "deals" gets a score of 1,052. However, that doesn't tell the whole story of the importance of these particular carewords. When I checked with Overture, a company that sells search-based ads, I found that in February 2006 the following searches were made in the U.S. market:

Search phrase	Number of searches
Vacation deals	17,623
Vacation special offers	0
Travel special offers	46
Travel deals	58,615
Cheap travel	90,679

There are a number of interesting points here. Firstly, hardly anyone searches using the words "special offers" – there were 17,623 people who searched for "vacation deals" in February 2006, but not a single person who searched for "vacation special offers."

as examples of the Long Tail—much more variety can be offered on the Web than in traditional book and music stores.

The Long Tail is an interesting theory and for certain environments it has major implications. However, I have unfortunately found Long Tail theory being used as an excuse of the put-it-upper. "Let's just put everything up on our website because everything is of interest to somebody."

There is value in the Long Tail but it is in the Long Neck where the most condensed profit and value lies. The good manager is focused on ensuring that, first and foremost, the Long Neck is as polished and as perfected as possible.

But what does this Long Neck theory actually mean? Well, let's look at the tourism example again. If you were managing Great Irish Holidays, you would want to make sure you did two things really well:

have a great accommodation booking process
have lots of excellent special offers

There is a Long Neck to every website I have ever examined—a core essence of what customers want from it. Unfortunately, too many websites that I have dealt with do not understand the essence of what they do. Don't make that mistake. Understanding what your website is about and perfecting those core tasks is how you deliver maximum value.

7 KILLER HEADINGS AND SUMMARIES

"Most people just look at the first couple of words and only read on if they are engaged by those words," according to *Eyetrack III*. "For headlines – especially longer ones – it would appear that the first couple of words need to be real attention-grabbers if you want to capture eyes."

"The same goes for blurbs [summaries] – perhaps even more so," the study continues. "Our findings about blurbs suggest that, not only should they be kept short, but the first couple of words need to grab the viewer's attention."

YOUR HEADING MUST HAVE PUNCH

Your heading (headline, title) is the single most important thing you will write on the Web. For the impatient scan-reader, your heading is your hook. It is the ultimate killer content – that first vital connection with your reader – so it must mean business.

If you want to reach the impatient scan-reader, your headings should adhere to the following rules.

1. Be compelling
- **If your heading is compelling enough it can break every rule in the book; some of the most compelling headings break lots of rules.**
- **Use carewords. Get the readers' carewords into your heading. The heading is the first and most important device you have to lock in your reader.**
- **Always lead with the need. Avoid starting a heading from**

your point of view or from the point of view of the organization you are writing for.

- Never congratulate yourself; congratulate your reader. If you don't engage the interest – that is, the self-interest – of the reader, you fail. So don't say "It's our 50th anniversary: 50% off." Instead, say "50% off: it's our 50th anniversary."
- Consider using the second person – "you" – in your headings. Sometimes, it can be good to frame it in a question: "Do you want to learn . . .?"
- Be positive – generally, people respond better to positive statements. Occasionally, though, the negative can work. The heading "Do you make these mistakes in Web writing?" has been known to work.
- A heading shouldn't read like a sentence: a sentence should flow, but a heading should stop you and grab your attention. To make a heading work, you should strip away all those redundant words. For example, "What is real on the Internet is not always clear" is a sentence, but "What's real on Internet not always clear" is a heading.

2. Be clear

- Avoid Shakespearean allusions and esoteric puns; get to the point. Tell readers exactly what they are going to get if they read on. However, rhyming or alliteration (see our old favorite, "Retire Rich") can be very effective, providing the message is still compelling.

3. Be complete

- A heading often has to stand on its own on a homepage or in a search result. So it should be complete – it should make sense on its own.

4. Be concise

- **A heading should consist of eight words or fewer. Reading is like breathing. Think of a heading as a short, sharp intake of breath. It should have impact – you can't achieve that with too many words.**

5. Be correct

- **A heading sets up an expectation of what the readers will get if they read on, so you've got to deliver on that expectation. In journalism, there is the concept of "bait and switch," where the heading promises something and the story doesn't deliver. If you bait and switch, you will lose the trust of your reader.**

HEADINGS SHOULD STAND ON THEIR OWN TWO FEET

What does the following heading mean to you?

A crushing burden on industry

Would it be clearer if you read the associated summary?

"European Union requirements will present an opportunity for specialist companies. Manufacturers, however, are less optimistic."

What are manufacturers less optimistic about? The above heading and summary are unclear and incomplete. They appeared in the *Financial Times* newspaper in September 2002. Beside them was a very large picture of computers being recycled. Get it? A "crushing burden" is a clever play on recycling.

This sort of word play can work well in a print environment because you control the context. Your heading, summary, picture, and body text are set in ink. They are fixed on the page. When you look at a print page, research indicates that the first thing you focus on is the picture, *then* you move to the text. However, research indicates that the opposite is true of the Web, and I believe one reason for this is that, on the Web, the text downloads faster than the image.

Killer headings make for bestsellers.

Headings are very important aids to classification. If you worked in a bookshop, where do you think you would place the book by Donald Norman entitled *The Psychology of Everyday Things*. Would you put it in the psychology section? A lot of staff did, even though it was a book on design.

Some people came into bookshops, feeling a bit down and looking for a book that would help them through their depression. They flicked through *The Psychology of Everyday Things* and felt even more depressed. Tears began to flow as they muttered, "I'll never be able to design these beautiful things." They threw the book down, and left the shop very upset. The book's sales were somewhat miserable too.

When the next edition came out, the book was renamed *The Design of Everyday Things* – much clearer. It became a bestseller. (And people leaving bookshops were less depressed.) One word made all the difference, and the world was a happier place.

TEST TO FIND YOUR KILLER HEADING

There is a science to writing headings. It is not a hard science but it is a science nonetheless. Basically, some headings grab attention; some headings don't. I collected a list of headings covering the launch of the Apple iTunes online music service. I gave this list to over 1,500 people in Iceland, Ireland, Finland, Norway, Italy, Taiwan, Hong Kong, Singapore, New Zealand, Australia, Slovenia, Sweden, and the U.S. Out of the 31 headings, 22% of the people chose this heading:

Tons of tunes

And 18% chose this heading:

Apple iTunes sells million-plus songs in a week

Both these headings were much more popular than the others. The most popular one, "Tons of Tunes," is very short, uses alliteration, and holds lots of promise. It's inviting and it is clear: you will get tons of tunes if you click here.

The second most popular heading — "Apple iTunes sells million-plus songs in a week" – is packed full of information. It is clear and concise. It's got real punch. It's compelling: Wow! A million-plus songs in a week – must be good; I'd better read more.

The following heading didn't receive a single vote from anybody:

Apple's music store breaks the mold and sells technology

From this heading, you don't even know if it's an online or offline store. The heading is also inaccurate, as iTunes doesn't sell technology; it sells music. It also misses the point: people don't buy technology – they buy music.

An important point to understand here is that, while some headings are obviously flawed, it is very difficult – even for a professional writer – to decide what the killer heading is. That's why you need to test your headings to find out which one has the killer touch.

WRITE KILLER SUMMARIES

If the heading is the hook, the summary is the line that pulls you in. The summary gives readers all the information they need to decide whether to read on or not.

The summary should lead with the need.

Keep the following in mind when writing summaries:

- **Sell. The summary should answer the question "What's in it for me?".**
- **Focus on the Who, What, Where, When, and How.**
- **Include compelling carewords.**
- **The last sentence should have real punch. Journalists are taught that the best way to end a summary is with a dramatic sentence such as "And then the shit hit the fan."**
- **Keep your summaries to 30 words or fewer. (I used to say 50 words or fewer, but I think the 50-word summary is more the exception than the rule on the Web these days.)**

It takes a long time to get really good at writing great summaries and headings. You need to practice, practice, practice. Focus on the facts and on what is compelling. Remember that the heading and summary should communicate a clear message on their own.

Another trick is to write the summary last. Get at least a first draft down of the whole content, and then work on the summary. That way, it'll be easier to find the killer line in the killer content.

I collected a list of 17 summaries based on the Apple iTunes launch story and had over 2,000 people from 13 countries quickly choose their favorite. Practically everywhere, one summary was chosen above any other. The first sentence of this summary began "**99 cents per download, no restrictions.**" In fact, it received 49% of all votes. This is an amazing result. The top three summaries represented 68% of votes, and the bottom seven summaries represented less than 3%. Out of the 13 countries where the test was carried out, the "99 cents per download" summary was first by a wide margin in 12 of them (in the 13th country, it was second).

Across cultures, people reacted in the same way. They responded to communication that spoke in a clear and compelling manner to what they really cared about. They also responded to a classic marketing technique – it has long been known that, if you want to grab attention, 99 is a magic number. (Think of £4.99, $99.99, etc.)

Out of over 2,000 people in 13 different countries, only two – yes, *two* – people voted for the summary that had this first sentence: **"The music industry owes a lot to technology."**

YOU ARE NOT THE CENTER OF THE UNIVERSE

Interestingly, the heading and the summary that nobody was interested in both emphasize technology. Very few people care about technology – it's just a tool. People do care about cheap music that is easy to purchase and has no restrictions in relation to how they listen to it.

The technology industry – like every other industry – thinks that it is the center of the universe, and loves to write as if it were. However, people like Mary, Tomas, Johan, and Peter and Joan McBride don't really care about the technology, pharmaceutical, investment, or tourism industries. They care about their own needs and the needs of those they care about.

Don't write to flatter your own ego. It can be a fatal mistake to think that what *you* care about most is what you reader cares about most. You sell yourself, your product, your service, your idea, or your beliefs by first and foremost connecting with what your audience really cares about.

Aristotle was a very smart philosopher, but he got a couple of things wrong – including the proposition that our lovely green Earth was at the center of the universe and that everything else revolved around us. This is a very human misconception, of course, and one that it took us a long time to get over.

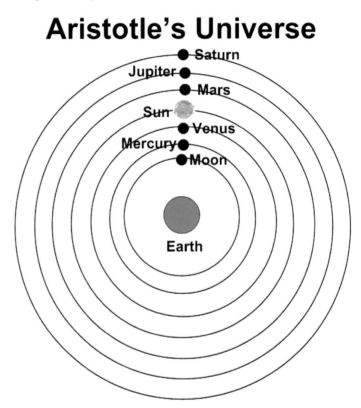

Every book should have a yoga moment – a moment of calm meditation and enlightenment – and this is the yoga moment of *Killer Web Content*. Please focus on the image of Aristotle's universe, in particular, on the image of the Earth.

Now replace the word *Earth* with the name of your organization (or if you don't work for an organization, with your own name).
Now say this out loud, like a mantra:

We – are – not – the – center – of – the – universe.

Repeat this three times before you start work on your Web content, and you are much more likely to create killer instead of filler.

TIPS FOR KILLER SENTENCES AND PARAGRAPHS

If headings are a short intake of breath, sentences should read like comfortable breathing. They should be easy on the eye and thus should be 20 words or fewer. Try to make just one point with each sentence, and make sure that the carewords are at the beginning of the sentence, rather than at the end. Be clear. Be concise.

Web paragraphs should ideally be 70 words or fewer, which is roughly four sentences. Always start the paragraph with the strongest sentence and start the strongest sentence with the strongest careword. Remember, if that sentence doesn't catch your readers' attention, they will scan the first sentence of the next paragraph or hit the "Back" button.

Never have a dead-end for Web content.

On the Web, you must have an ending to your content that is a call to action. Good Web content is always task-focused, and the best ending allows your customers to go about completing their tasks. So, write the links that lead to completion:

- **Buy now while stocks last**
- **Fill in the tax exemption form now**
- **Talk to one of our experts**
- **Book your place at the workshop**
- **Get more information on the speaker**

- **See what other customers are saying**
- **Learn how to get your friends involved**

TEST, TEST, TEST

No matter how good you are as a writer, it will be almost impossible for you to know what is killer Web content unless you test. This is particularly true for headings and summaries. In this sense, Web content is not all that different from direct mail marketing.

Professional direct mail marketers will always send out a selection of sample letters before they do the mass mailshot. There will be slight variations in each of the sample letters – a slightly different heading, summary, final paragraph, etc. Some letters will get a better response than others, and if the marketer is lucky, one of them will really hit pay-dirt. This will be the killer content.

There has never been a better medium to discover killer content than the Web. True, most organizations do a bad job at measuring the value of their Web content, but the potential is there, and progressive organizations are testing that potential. I mentioned the technique of split-testing in Chapter 2 – whichever way you decide to measure content, make sure you test it again and again. (You can test your headings and summaries using the same careword finder technique described in the previous chapter.)

An executive in Microsoft told me that Microsoft tested these two headings:

10 smart tips for using PowerPoint
10 key tips for using PowerPoint

and that the second one had three times the click-through rate of the first. Changing one word increased the click-through rate by a factor of three. One word.

8 TO BLOG OR NOT TO BLOG?

Blogging is a conversation. It has become a phenomenon because people love to communicate. It allows you to get closer to your audience, because when you say something they can respond back with what they think. In fact, the audience may well lead the conversation at times by suggesting new ideas.

From the organization's perspective, blogging can have two key benefits:

1. **In an intranet, it can allow more and better conversations between staff, particularly between staff who are in different physical locations, and/or who are at different levels within the organization. It can thus break down hierarchies and silo-thinking.**

2. **It can establish a powerful interaction between the organization and the customer. A good blog can show that you are listening and responding to the needs of your customers. A good blog can make your customers part of the product development process.**

From a personal perspective, blogging is like an extended CV. At a very basic level, a blog says "I exist and I have something to say." At a more practical level a blog says "I exist, I have something smart to say, give me a (better) job, please."

"Blog" is a combination of two words: "web" and "log." It is a Web-based diary or journal. Some blogs are focused on the personal writing of the author; they are, in essence, an online diary. Others take an editorial approach. Editors trawl the Web for interesting content and might then write up a short comment and link to this content, or simply cut and paste the heading and summary from the original webpage, while also providing a link to it.

Blogs reflect a passion to communicate.

They say there's a book inside everybody. Well, the blog lets the book out! Bloggers, the writers and editors of blogs, are people with attitude. They have a passion to communicate. You can't have a good blog if you can't write well or if you don't have well-formulated opinions.

An example of a blog

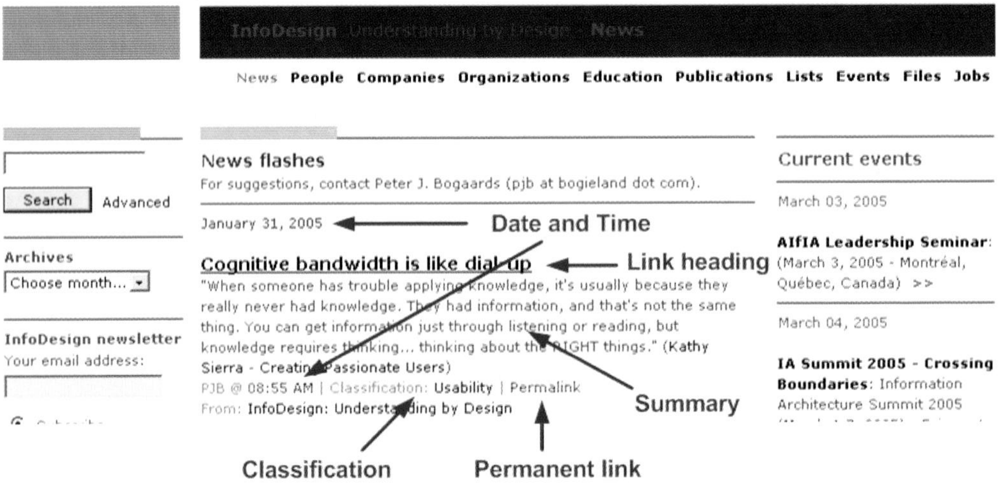

The InfoDesign blog shown above focuses on information design and is a blog I find useful. The image, taken from that blog, shows how a classic blog entry is structured:

- **Date and Time: A key distinguishing feature of blogs is that each piece of content is dated.**
- **Link heading: A typical blog entry will link to another**

piece of content on the Web. (The diary-like blogs don't always do this.)

- **Summary: Blog entries tend to be short and punchy; so the general rules of Web content you'll find in *Killer Web Content* are ideal for writing blogs.**
- **Classification: A classification structure is important for blogs especially as they grow bigger. Otherwise, it becomes difficult find older articles. The InfoDesign example blog post is classified under "usability." (I'll be dealing with classification design in Chapter 12.)**
- **Permanent link: Blogs have a feature called "permalink." This gives the blog post a unique website address so that it can be directly linked to.**

BLOGGING IS PART OF THE TEXT REVOLUTION

Who would have thought that in 2005 *Fortune* magazine would have chosen blogging — plain old editing and writing — as the number one tech trend? Let's not get carried away, though. While blogging is an interesting trend in communication, it is simply a new part of the communications mix.

The similarities between the music and technology industries are striking. Each one desperately needs a "next big thing." Each one desperately needs to whip up a frenzy about something that is definitely going to change the world – until the next big thing comes along.

Blogs are the latest "next big thing" which is going to change everything, according to some pundits. They're going to bring big corporations to their knees and give ultimate power to the consumer and independent advocate. And these pundits have at least one real-life story to back up their latest pet theory.

"Heard about what bloggers did to Kryptonite?" they ask. Well, in September 2004, someone blogged that you could open a Kryptonite lock with a BIC pen. This claim was quickly verified by other bloggers.

The Kryptonite Bike Lock Company responded lamely by saying that the locks were still a "deterrent to theft." The bloggers were infuriated and lambasted Kryptonite. Finally, Kryptonite was forced to recall the lock, costing an estimated ten million dollars.

At least, that's what became the popular myth. And a nice little story it makes too. But is it the truth? Kryptonite claimed it was aware of what was happening on the Internet from day one, and that it worked flat out to come up with a solution. The truth of the story – as usual – is probably a bit more complicated than the bloggers or Kryptonite would like you to believe.

Almost exactly ten years earlier, in the autumn of 1994, a bug was discovered in the Intel Pentium processor. Someone published information on this bug on the Web and the story began to get picked up. Intel initially ignored the criticism, claiming that the bug only occurred in rare circumstances, which was true. However, the controversy just grew and grew. Finally, Intel relented, with Andrew Grove, then CEO, stating, "The past few weeks have been deeply troubling. What we view as an extremely minor technical problem has taken on a life of its own." A no-questions-asked return policy was announced. (Hardly anyone took it up.)

If you're not listening to what bloggers are saying about you, you're not doing your job as a professional communicator.

Intel didn't *listen*. Kryptonite may or may not have listened. Communication has changed. Many organizations are used to a one-way system, broadcasting a message to an audience. However, the Web gives today's consumers an opportunity to talk back in a way that was not possible before; the communications mix has become two-way. And that's going to really shake up a lot of communications and marketing departments, because, let's face it, most organizations are simply not used to pesky consumers talking back.

However, let's not lose sight of the fact that Intel is still around, as are most of the other so-called dinosaurs that the Web was supposed to obliterate. The irony of the Web is that, while on the one hand it gives a voice to the individual consumer, it also rewards size and scale. The Web may have millions of websites, but it is dominated by a small number of mega-sites. And, as we will see in the next chapter, they are likely to get bigger and stronger as the Web matures.

THE ADVANTAGES OF BLOGS TO THE ORGANIZATION

Blogs tend to be personal and conversational, and I will look at why you, as a professional, should consider blogging later in the chapter. However, here I'd like to examine the potential advantages of blogs to the organization.

- **A human face**

  Modern organizations are creating greater distances between themselves and their consumers. Self-service, automation, and outsourcing all reduce the number of opportunities – the touch points – the organization has to interact with the consumer. When the consumer can't put a "face" on an organization, it's easy to see that organization as a soulless entity. Blogging has the potential to give it a human face.

- **A finger on the pulse**

  A key component of blogging is that people can easily post replies to any comment the blogger makes. If an organization is prepared to listen, it can spot trends – negative and positive – early, and respond appropriately to them. Done well, blogs can become a part of the product development process, helping ensure that the new product or service is addressing real customer needs. Blogs can be a wonderful source of market research, of new ideas, and of feedback.

A great blog is a window into the mind of a great thinker.

- ● **A sharing culture**
  Intranet blogs can be an excellent way to share and explore ideas, product concepts, etc., within an organization. They can be a way of knitting virtual teams together whose individual members may live on different continents. Some organizations – such as Google, for example – use them to document product developments for patent application purposes.

THE DISADVANTAGES OF BLOGS TO THE ORGANIZATION

Blogs are no magic formula for success and can have drawbacks, including the following.

- ● **Blogs require talented writers**
  There may well be a book inside everybody but the stark truth is that many people don't have very much to say and what they do have to say they say badly. I have sometimes found that the people who have the most time to write have the least to say, and that the people who have the most to say don't have enough time to write it down. Thus, the real expertise within an organization can lay hidden beneath a pile of trivia. Blogs can be a wonderful way of wasting time at work.

- ● **Blogs are open to abuse**
  The very strength of blogging is that it is individual rather than organization-focused. So the organization that wants to allow public blogging needs to tread a very careful line between keeping

on message and allowing freedom of expression. It's nice that a blogger has an independent voice, but how far can an employee go in criticizing the organization just to show that independence?

It's nice to be open and transparent, but what sort of information is an employee allowed to publish? These are not simple questions. Companies such as Kmart, Delta, and Google have fired staff because it was believed that confidential information was posted in their blogs.

It is a misconception to think that because blogs are written by individuals they are more credible. Often, the reverse is so.

Because blogs tend to be the voice of an individual, a "real" person, some believe that they are more authentic than the voice of the organization. However, the individual voice is just as open to abuse as that of the organization. There are numerous stories of people being paid to pretend to be independent. In truth, we all have prejudices; it's just that some of us are better at hiding them than others.

In some cases, the blogger is a fiction. For over three years, thousands of people followed the blog of Plain Layne, a lesbian from Minnesota. It turned out Plain Layne was actually a 35-year-old male entrepreneur from Minnesota.

For all its virtues, the Web can be the land of the scam. "Ten Years, Ten Trends," a 2004 study by the Center for the Digital Future, found that:

- **Although the Web has become an important source of information, the initially high level of credibility of information on the Web began to drop in 2003, and declined even further in 2004.**
- **Websites by established media were trusted by 74% of survey respondents and government websites were trusted by 73%. But websites by individuals – that includes blogs – were trusted by only 9%.**

Building credibility and trust takes time, so don't expect that if you launch a blog it will be an overnight success. Blogging is a form of publishing and most publications that do succeed generally take many years to build up a regular readership. You must be willing to put in quality blogging time week in, week out. A good idea might take up one paragraph but could have taken a day or more to research and think through.

When blogging, remember that the Web has a long memory. Do not publish any material on your blog on impulse. Ask these questions:

- **Who might read it? Suppose a prospective employer or customer reads it, what would they think?**
- **In what ways might it be interpreted?**
- **How will it stand up in a year? In five years?**
- **How will it further my career?**

GET YOUR OWN WEBSITE

The real advantages of blogging are for individuals like you. You must publish today about the important things you do if you are ambitious. Publishing is about visibility. It's about getting your name in front of those who matter to you. If you do something great and don't create a record of what you did, did you really do it? As far as the Web is concerned, you didn't, and the Web is becoming *the* global memory. So you've got to get it down – get it recorded.

Academia may look somewhat mild and comradely to an outsider, but it is an intensely competitive environment, governed by the law "publish or perish." Ambitious and creative academics get published and not-so-ambitious and not-so-creative ones get forgotten. Take Albert Einstein, for example: he gained fame and influence not after he formulated his theories on relativity, but after he *published* them.

We have moved from lifelong employment to lifelong learning, and the organization has become, in part, like a university. The implications are clear: as members of this lifelong learning university, we will be expected to publish more in order to show what we have learned and to share the best of that learning.

A personal website is the universal passport of the knowledge society.

In the past, many people gave their loyalty to an organization in the hope that it would give them lifelong employment and fulfillment. That's rarely the case anymore, and the implication is that you will need to publish outside the organization so that others will become aware of your abilities. You must look after yourself today, and your blog or other type of website is a way of saying that you are always open to new opportunities. You should never be too busy to look after your long-term interests.

Get your own URL (website address), because your website should be one of the most permanent things you carry with you throughout your life. You may change careers, houses, or even countries, but your website address and its associated e-mail address shouldn't change.

E-MAIL NEWSLETTERS

It's not just Web publishing you should focus on, of course. The more places you can get your name published, the better; so if there are offline magazines or newspapers that will take your copy, so much the better.

Personally, I don't blog but I've been writing a weekly e-mail newsletter called *New Thinking* for ten years, which I also publish on my website. I follow the same schedule every week and I have never missed an issue. People ask me how I manage to do that. I ask them how they manage to get up on a Monday morning. Do I always feel excited by writing? No. Am I always brimming with ideas? No. I just tell my brain – in a very determined manner – that I must write my newsletter every week. And somehow, regardless of all sorts of problems, I manage to get it published.

Despite the huge increase in spam, I would estimate that 85% of my business results from subscribers to my newsletter. It's like this: people come to my website; they might read a bit of content; they might think it's good; and they might intend to come back – but most never do. Now, if I can get them to join a newsletter, well then I can regularly reach them.

Most of my clients spend an average of 12 months as subscribers to my newsletter first before they make an initial contact. That way, they get to know what I'm about and what my particular angle is. Often, what happens is that I get hired by people who are of a like mind to me. They've been saying the same things within their organizations and believe that, if they can bring in an outside voice, it will add momentum and credibility to their views.

My e-mail newsletter is a perfect way for me to find the right client. It is a very simple text-only newsletter, as you can see from the image opposite, but it helps me get to work with some of the world's best organizations, allowing me to charge high fees and deliver real value. (You can subscribe to *New Thinking* by going to www.gerrymcgovern.com.)

```
*******************************************************************
NEW THINKING NEW THINKING NEW THINKING NEW THINKING NEW THINKING
By Gerry McGovern - http://www.gerrymcgovern.com
*******************************************************************
January 31, 2005 - Volume 10 Number 05
*******************************************************************

PUBLISHER SOUGHT FOR BOOK ON WEB CONTENT
Do you think that 2005 is going to be the year of web content
(from websites to blogs)? I do, and I'm writing a book full of
powerful research and insight. Drop me an email if you'd like to
find out more.
<mailto:gerry@gerrymcgovern.com>

*******************************************************************
DO YOU MAKE THE MOST COMMON MISTAKE IN CONTENT MANAGEMENT?

The biggest mistake in content management is writing for the
organization and not for the reader. It is one of the hardest
mistakes to correct, but there are ways to ensure that you don't
make it.

For millions of years, humans trusted only themselves and the
small group or family around them. The 'fight or flight'
instinct dictated that you either ran from or killed a stranger.
It is the most natural thing in the world to distrust the
stranger, and it is a very modern idea to trust them. (The book,
The Company of Strangers, is well worth reading if you're
interested in this area.)
```

I don't have a blog because the weekly newsletter covering a single theme works well for me and I have been doing it for nearly ten years now, so I'm a bit stuck in my ways. You don't have to blog, nor do you have to have an e-mail newsletter, but you do need to publish, because otherwise you are invisible on the Web.

Really Simple Syndication (RSS) allows you to get your favorite blogs, e-mail newsletters, or other Web content delivered directly to your desktop. So, instead of going to all your favorite websites to check what's new, you can instruct your RSS aggregator to download new content from these websites as it is published.

For the marketer and communicator, RSS is just another tool to allow consumers get content *exactly* the way they want it. RSS puts people more in control. They find their favorite Web content and then get it delivered to them on a regular basis.

RSS allows you as the reader to pick and choose. You could decide to download just headlines from a selection of websites, for example, or you could classify the content you want to receive so that it's all nicely organized when you go to read it. It's an information-overloaded world, and RSS helps some of us swim instead of sink.

If you're a marketer or communicator, you might be thinking that this all sounds very technical. Sure, there are technical issues relating to blogs, e-mail newsletters, and RSS, but you're just going to have to get a handle on them. To say "I'm not technical" in this day and age is just not going to cut it, unless you plan to retire in the next five years.

However, the essence of all that is going on on the Web is still communication: two-way communication. The technical stuff is there, and we need to be comfortable with it, but it's still the content that is important and, as we'll see in the next chapter, getting that content found.

9 SEARCH: HOW TO GET FOUND

Every day, millions of people search on the Web, and if your content is not on the first page of the search results, you might as well not exist for many of them. A study by a search specialist company called Mondosoft says that only one person in 20 goes to the second page of search results. I've read other studies that say that, if you're not in the first three pages or, at most, the first five pages, forget about it.

It's a jungle out there. The Web is a tough marketplace, with an awful lot of competition to get onto the first page of search results. However, there are long-term strategies that you can pursue that will maximize your chances of getting onto that first page.

WRITE FOR HOW PEOPLE SEARCH

You need not so much to understand the search engines but to understand how people search. A big focus in the search marketing industry is "search engine optimization," but I think this is the wrong long-term focus. Such an approach can result in tactics that try to trick the search engines by creating content that ranks well with them; it will, however, be a big turn-off for the reader because it has no style or flow.

The content of the imaginary tourism website Canadian Vacations illustrated overleaf (and paraphrased from an actual website) is written very much from a search engine optimization perspective. It will work well with many search engines because it repeats a lot of carewords ("Canada," "vacations," "weekend break," etc.), and because of how these words are positioned in the content.

Canadian Vacations, Weekends and Weekend Breaks in Canada

Canadian vacations, weekends and weekend breaks in Canada—with such a large selection of vacations to choose from you won't find a better deal.

If you are planning a Canadian weekend break away or a vacation to Canada, you will find a multitude of special vacation offers and breaks waiting for you. From luxury hotels, to self-catering apartments, Canada is the premier destination for exquisite vacations and breaks.

So while this content might help bring someone to the website, it might then turn that person off because it reads in an unnatural and pushy manner. There is a middle ground – a way to write content that reads well and also works well with search engines – and that's what this chapter is about.

Getting somebody to click on your search result is just the first step.

Search engines try to understand why and how people search; so, if you publish content that people are searching for, you are also optimizing your content for search engines. Always remember that the task of your customer is not simply to find you in a search engine – that's just the first step. To complete the task, they need to be able to do something on your website: to buy something, to download something, to contact somebody.

Again, it comes down to carewords. The searcher is a hunter-gatherer who thinks in carewords, using them to track the scent of information.

When people are searching, they tend to write between one and three carewords into the search box. If you want to reach them, you need to know what those words are and use them appropriately in your content. If you don't, you could end up with frustrated readers or not enough customers, as the two stories below illustrate.

When searching for information on outer space, readers of the BBC (British Broadcasting Corporation) website don't use the words "solar system" or '"space." Instead, they generally use "planets." However, for a long time, the main reference to planets on the BBC website was a television show about the sea called "The Blue Planet." So people were trying to get into outer space and ending up in the sea!

A luxury hotel group wrote about its "deluxe hotels" on its website, but the problem was that 40 times more people search for "luxury hotels" than "deluxe hotels." Writing about deluxe hotels is nice marketing jargon but it's not how people search, and if you want to get found by search engines, you need to use your customers' words, not yours.

Find out about how people search and you get a window into how they think.

The Web offers us this wonderful ability to find out how people are searching. This, in essence, is a window into their minds, helping us to understand what they are thinking and what they care about.

Don't be an earthworm – get linked.

When researchers achieved the final count of the number of genes in the human body, they were surprised and somewhat disappointed. It turned out that humans don't have all that many "more" genes than the lowly earthworm.

What made humans "human," though, was not so much the number of genes but rather the *number of connections* between them. The human body is a big family of genes with multiple relationships.

There is nothing search engines prefer more than killer Web content.

When pursuing a Web-linking strategy, keep the following in mind:

● **Killer Web content gets killer Web links**

One of the main reasons the first ten links are to me when you search for "Gerry McGovern" on Google, Yahoo, or MSN is because I actively encourage people to republish some of my content, once they credit me and *link* back to me. I do this regularly with my e-mail newsletter, *New Thinking*. It's a great way of getting links and getting my name quoted on other websites.

● **Link within your discipline**

As a general rule, get linked from websites within your particular discipline. This is important for two reasons:

1. **The more people see you linked to within a particular discipline, the more impressed they are likely to be, as Web linking is akin to word-of-mouth. If people see links to you on lots of other websites, that's a major credibility builder.**

2. **Search engines like to find logical patterns and groupings for links, and tend to reward you if you are well linked in a particular pattern once the person is searching for a careword related to that pattern. (This is not always the case, however, as we will see below at "Strengthen your weak ties.")**

● **Don't focus overly on the hubs**

In a network, a hub is a site, such as Yahoo, Google, Microsoft, or Amazon, that has a lot of links coming into it. It's great to get links from these hubs. However, especially when you're starting out, it may be very difficult to get such links. Sometimes, it can be a clever strategy not to focus too much on getting linked through major hubs but to focus more on minor hubs that still have the capacity to deliver value.

● **Strengthen your weak ties**

A study was done on how a group of people found work, and the results showed that a friend of a friend was more likely to have got them that important job introduction than family members and close friends. There are all sorts of reasons for this. For starters, you have more friends of friends than you have friends. It can be very comfortable to get links from websites you admire and from websites in your peer group, but these might not be the websites your customers are frequenting. You don't want to be getting links from websites that have nothing to do with your business, but you do need to think outside the box, and, of course, to keep thinking about which websites your reader is going to.

● **Go for quality, not quantity**

There might be short-term benefits from search engines for getting lots of low quality links, through reciprocal linking and other, more dubious practices, of which there are many. However, just as you should write content for people who search rather than for a search engine, you should get links that are likely to impress your potential customers rather than simply garner some short-term benefit from a search engine. One link from a well-regarded website could bring you far more business (whether or not search engine traffic) than a hundred from lesser-known websites. Less is more.

● **Be careful about reciprocal linking**

The "you give me a link and I'll give you a link" approach is the easiest – though usually least effective – way to get linked. If their link is dependent on you giving them a reciprocal link, be careful. Unless linking to them provides real value for your reader, don't do it. Remember, every time you provide an external link, you provide one more exit point from your website, and, if you put up too many exit points, people will leave.

● **Get linked from websites that don't link much**
If you are one of the few links from a prestigious website, then that says a lot. Some search engines will give you an extra boost for a link from such a website.

● **Get linked from important Web directories**
This is particularly important if you have a new website. Initially it can take quite a while to get search engines to index (*spider*) you, and you will certainly increase your chances if you can be found in important directories, such as DMOZ and Yahoo. Here are some points to keep in mind.
  - **"It's important to read each directory's FAQ and follow it precisely," Jill Whalen of Highrankings.com states. "Making mistakes in the submission process could cost you dearly, as directory listings are difficult to change later in the game."**
  - **Of course, it's not just the major directories you need to focus on. There may be specialist directories in your discipline that will be well worth getting listed on.**
  - **Don't go overboard. There are also thousands and thousands of directories that have few or no visitors and are really not worth the effort.**

● **Get linked with the right carewords**
Try to get links that use the most important carewords of your readers. If you offer cheap flights to Dublin, make sure that sites link to you with text that says something like "Best cheap flights to Dublin." If you have great content on heart disease symptoms, the link you get should read something like "Heart disease symptoms: the five most important." A link is like a signpost, and as soon as a reader sees a link that includes their carewords, they are much more likely to click.

151

So if you were writing about heart disease symptoms, here's how you might write the heading and summary.

- **Heart disease symptoms**
  Heart disease symptoms need to be recognized as early as possible. Early treatment of heart ailments can save lives. Here are the most important heart disease symptoms to look out for.

- **Use exact careword phrases**
  Certain carewords are going to be extremely competitive; so slight refinements can make a big difference. Content management solutions is an area I specialize in. At one stage, when I searched for "content management solutions" in Google, I was on the first page of search results. However, when I searched for "content management solution," I was nowhere to be found. I changed the content a little on my pages, so that I used the singular "solution" as well as the plural, and in time I ranked well for both phrases. (As a general rule, people tend to search for the plural more than the singular.)

- **Measure careword density**
  What we're talking about here is the number of times that a particular careword is mentioned in your text. Consider the following:

  - **In the heading and summary on heart disease symptoms that I used earlier, there are a total of 30 words, nine of which are the carewords "heart disease symptoms." This gives a careword density for this text of approximately 26%. This is very high (but not unacceptable) in such a small quantity of text.**
  - **Over 250-500 words of text, say, the keyword density should be in the region of 3–5%. What is critical here is how the content reads. If you put too many carewords in the text, it will lack flow and will likely**

read as hype. If that happens, then most readers will just hit the "Back" button.

- If you write a very long text, you will generally find that it is hard to maintain a reasonable careword density, as it is generally hard to maintain a focus on a particular set of carewords over a long piece of text. This is another reason why you should keep your content short and focus on a single idea.
- Have no more than three carewords (or careword phrases) per page.

● **Use emphasis where appropriate**

Search engines give a little extra value to content that uses emphasis. Embolden your headings and summaries. (Alternatively, you can use the <H> tag for your headings.) Some advocate the use of italics. However, italics are hard to read on a screen. (They make the text look as if it is having a nervous breakdown.) Remember always to put the reader first, not the search engine.

● **Get your carewords into your links**

Write your hypertext links like you write headings – get those carewords in. Search engines give special emphasis to words found in links. Avoid using phrases such as "click here" and "download now," as people don't search for expressions like these.

HOW TO WRITE GREAT TITLE TAGS

As well as the critical importance of linking and visible page content, the title tag is another really important factor that most search engines use to rank a webpage.

Every page on your website should have a unique title tag. What often happens is that a generic title tag is written, and then it is used again and again, as in the following example, a sample search results page for Whitehouse.gov. (This is one of the most common mistakes that occur on websites; so I'd advise you to go and check your own website.)

What happens when you repeat the title tag

Press Briefing by Ari Fleischer ◀━━━━ TITLE

For Immediate Release Office of the **Press** Secretary January 9, 2003. **Press Briefing** by Ari Fleischer James S. Brady **Press Briefing** Room. ...
www.whitehouse.gov/news/ releases/2003/01/20030109-8.html - 74k - Cached - Similar pages

Press Briefing by Ari Fleischer

<a href="/news/releases/2003/03/20030321-pb.v.smil"></a>Watch Friday's **Press Briefing** with White House **Press** Secretary Ari Fleischer. ... **Press Briefing** view. ...
www.whitehouse.gov/news/ releases/2003/03/20030321-9.html - 80k - Cached - Similar pages

Press Briefing by Ari Fleischer

<a href="/news/releases/2002/12/20021202-pb.a.ram"></a>Listen to Monday's **Press Briefing** with White House **Press** Secretary Ari Fleischer. ...
www.whitehouse.gov/news/ releases/2002/12/20021202-6.html - 71k - Cached - Similar pages

The title tag is not just useful for the search engine. It is also an extremely important aid for the person who is searching. The title is the first copy they will see in relation to a particular search result. It is also the link, and so it should be the most compelling piece of text, encouraging the reader to click. Many people will scan the title, and, if it doesn't look useful, their eyes will move to the next search result.

Here are some specific tips for writing title tags.

● **Lead with the most important careword for that particular page. Where practical, start off with what is specific about the page and move to what is general. Many websites begin their titles with their brands or organization names, and then follow with what is unique about the page. (This is a very common mistake, so check your website.) If, however, you know that a lot of people search for your brand name and that you are currently not appearing high in search results when that sort of search happens, then putting your brand name** as the first part of the title can be a good idea. This has its drawbacks, though, because people read from the specific to the general. They want to know about the page itself first, and then about the context of that the page. By starting with the general, you are slowing down their ability to comprehend.

● Write your title as you would write a heading. Keep it lean and mean. Strip away as many adjectives and unnecessary words as possible. The fewer words in a title, the greater stress a search engine will give to each particular word.

● Keep the title short. Don't have more than 60 characters (with spaces), which is roughly eight to ten words. Less is more. If you have longer titles than this, most search engines will truncate the text after the sixtieth character.

U2 Home Page: @U2 - U2 News, U2 Pix, U2 lyrics, U2 Collectors ... **◄——Truncated title**
@U2 provides U2 news, U2 photographs, U2 lyrics, and other U2 information in a non-profit, educational setting for anyone interested in learning about the ...
www.atu2.com/ - 39k - 1 Feb 2005 - Cached - Similar pages

The title of this website on U2 has been truncated because Google deems it too long. You will know a title has been truncated when you see an ellipsis (...) at the end of the text.

HOW TO WRITE A QUALITY DESCRIPTION TAG

While practically all search engines use the title tag as part of their results page, only some of them make use of the description tag in the two lines of text that usually come immediately after the title.

The Sydney Morning Herald: national, world, business ...
... [Garry Barker] Destra, Australia's largest supplier of online music, ...
opening in Australia of Apple's all-conquering iTunes Music Store. more ... **◄—— DESCRIPTION**
www.smh.com.au/ - Similar pages

159

Here are some tips for writing description tags:

- **Have a unique description tag for every page.**
- **Aim for a maximum of 200 characters (with spaces), which is about 30 words. If you can get away with fewer, do so. (If you have a summary on the page, then cut and paste that into the description tag.)**
- **Use the description to sell the page. Think of yourself as you scan a set of search results: a particular description has maybe one second to catch your eye before you move on. Well, if that's the way you scan a set of results, you can be pretty sure that's the way everyone else does too.**

HAVE LEAN, QUALITY HTML

The less HTML (Hypertext Mark-up Language) code you have, the better, as it makes it easier and faster for the search engine to index your page. One of the ways Google ensures that it downloads really fast is that it keeps its HTML really lean and mean. While images do represent most of a page's weight, HTML is also a factor; so keeping it tight will improve download speed.

Of course, lean, mean, fast-downloading pages are exactly what people want too. I would recommend that you should aim for a maximum of 50 KB (kilobytes) per page. (The Google homepage is about 11 KB.) Certainly, anything over 100 KB is going to be slow.

HAVE A SITE MAP

Strictly speaking, a site map presents two or three levels of your website in a map or organization-chart format. A site index, on the other hand, shows an A-Z list of how your website is classified. However, the words "map" and "index" have become interchangeable, with "site map" becoming the more popular of the two terms.

Search engine spiders like site maps/indexes because they allow them easily to go deeper into a website. Many people like site maps/indexes too, as they can have a quick scan of where the major sections of a website are.

Use a site map for smaller websites, and an index for larger ones. In fact, there's nothing wrong with offering both. Here are a couple of things to watch out for when designing site maps/indexes.

1. **When designing a site map, don't show it as a graphic, but rather lay it out as HTML.**

2. **Make sure that the site map/index is kept up to date. Out-of-date site maps/indexes are very annoying, both for your readers and the search spiders.**

FLASH CAUSES HEADACHES

I've nothing against Macromedia Flash design except for the fact that I generally detest it. All over the world, I have asked people what they do when they see a Flash intro. "Skip intro," they shout in unison. Where Flash is used to explain how a complicated product works or where it is used to save time in a process, it makes absolute sense. However, most Flash – particularly that found on a homepage – is a fourth-rate attempt to create TV ads by people who know they will never get the chance to create ones.

Search engines find it difficult to index a Flash-based website. This situation is improving and will no doubt improve even more, but the point still stands: search engines prefer text over Flash, and Flash-based websites – even if they could be indexed – usually have very little text, as they are image-driven.

BUILD YOUR WEBSITE TO APPEAR AS STATIC HTML

Dynamic webpages are pages that are not pre-built but that are built on the fly from a database whenever a person clicks on a link or makes some sort of selection. A typical use of dynamic content would be where you are requesting a flight to Washington DC at 3 p.m. on Tuesday with a particular airline. The airline website will send this query to the database and then build a dynamic page that will tell you if there are seats available and at what price.

Search engines have got much better at indexing content within databases. However, there can still be problems and it requires a lot of precision and expertise to get right. That means you need to make sure that your technical team focuses its energies on ensuring that the search engines won't have a problem indexing your website.

For a period, dynamic pages were really cool. It seemed that every IT department wanted its website to be dynamically built because that somehow said something about the quality of the website. The thinking was that if you had dynamic content you had quality content. Not so. If the content is badly written and out of date, then all that taking it from a database does is to make it dynamic badly written and out-of-date content. (Garbage in, garbage out.)

You don't need a dynamic website unless you have dynamic content needs, such as those of an airline. If your content doesn't change dynamically, then it is better to create a static HTML website. Of course, this website can be built from and maintained in a database or content management system, and you should be able to add new content whenever you want. (You may, in fact, have some dynamic content and some as static HTML.)

The advantages of having a static website are as follows:

- **You increase the search indexability of the website.**
- **Individual pages should be slightly faster to load, as they do not have to be called from a database.**
- **Your website will be cheaper to maintain because you will require less computing power.**

MANAGING FILES ON YOUR WEBSITE

Most search engines will index the popular file formats like Word and PDF. However, in many cases, you will need to do special work to ensure that a particular file type is search-engine friendly.

For many years, I have described this scenario to audiences: "Imagine you are on the Web, and you click on a link, a link that you think will bring you to an ordinary webpage. All of sudden, you are downloading a PDF. Do you feel excited?" Whether they are in Seattle, Sydney, or Singapore, very few feel excited; most feel annoyed.

People don't like wasting time on the Web. PDFs take more time to download than normal HTML pages. Many organizations use the PDF as a quick fix for their content – it's easier and quicker to put up a PDF than to publish the content properly in HTML. So, PDF often reflects a get-print-content-up-on-the-website-as-quickly-and-cheaply-as-possible approach. Another reason many people don't like PDFs is that the text is very hard to read on the screen, almost forcing you to print it out or risk a headache.

PDFs are useful for the following:

- **Long documents (1,000 words or more), as most people who need to read long documents prefer to print them out.**
- **Documents that have complicated layouts (lots of diagrams, forms, etc.).**

From a search engine optimization point of view, make sure PDFs – and other files – have appropriate title and description tags. If you have a long PDF, create a webpage with a summary in HTML. This serves two purposes:

tricks that are deliberately designed to fool the search engines, but nobody likes being made a fool of.

Short-term tactics that try to fool the search engines might well result in short-term gain, but can easily lead to long-term pain.

As I mentioned earlier, the keyword tag used to be important to search engines. But then the trick of stuffing the keyword tag with dozens of popular keywords became so common that most search engines began to downgrade its value. Now the tag will seldom if ever help your rankings.

Be very careful about taking the advice of those who promise you things that sound too good to be true, because – you know what? – they probably *are* too good to be true. You need to be very clear on what exactly you're getting into when employing search engine experts. Many of them are absolutely legitimate, but some employ shady practices that could in fact damage your website's reputation and ranking with the search engines. (Search engines have been known to punish and, on rare occasions, ban websites that tried to fool them too much.)

So, just like in ordinary business, the advice is: Keep it legitimate.

HOW TO HAVE A GOOD SEARCH EXPERIENCE FOR YOUR OWN WEBSITE

If you do all the things outlined so far in this chapter, you will significantly increase the chances of being ranked highly by the major public search engines (Google, Yahoo, AOL, and MSN Search). Should you have a search engine on your own website, you will also significantly increase the quality of its results.

For your own website, you're better to have no search engine than a bad one.

The question is: Do you actually need a search engine? If you have a relatively small website (less than 500 pages), then you probably don't. If you have very well-classified content that your readers feel comfortable navigating around, then you possibly don't need one either.

When I'm asked to analyze a website, one of the first things I do is what I call the "Google test." I browse for a while and find a random page on the website. I take a line of text from that page and put it into the search engine for that website. Then I put the same line of text in Google and get it to search within that website for that line of text. Usually, Google will find me the page quicker than the search engine of the website itself.

That's pretty amazing. Google indexes billions of pages. Unfortunately, it's because most organizations do a poor job of managing their own search engine process. How does your search engine shape up? Why not try the Google test?

I could go on and on about information overload, about how staff are very frustrated by intranet search engines, about how customers often turn to site-specific search as a last resort, knowing that the results they get back will most likely be rubbish. I'll stop. All I'll say is this: bad search is bad for business and bad for productivity. Fix your search engine or get rid of it.

Here are a number of things you can do to improve the quality of your search.

● **Search is a process not a project**
A search engine is not like some filing cabinet you buy, place in a corner, and forget about. Achieving quality search results is a process of observation and refinement. It is not at heart a technical issue but a publishing one, and you, as marketer and communicator, need to be actively involved on an ongoing basis if you really want to give a great search experience to your customers.

● **Watch out for trends**
If you have a lot of search activity on your website, then you should be analyzing it regularly for key trends. Are certain words being searched for much more than others? If so, maybe you need to use these words more in your content and navigation.

● **Nice wide search box**
One-word searches are still common, though the trend is towards two- and three-word searches. That requires a search box that is 25 to 30 characters wide. (It's very frustrating to have a tiny search box where you can only see half of what you are about to search for.) Here are some other tips regarding the search box:
  • **Do not place text in the search box.**
  • **If someone clicks on the search button without placing text in the search box, bring them to a dedicated search page. Alternatively, you could try publishing an error message saying: "Please place text in the search box, you idiot." On second thoughts, that's probably not a good idea.**

● **Search or Go button**
The text of the button to the right of the search box can be labeled "Search" or "Go." If using "Go," then you need to have

a heading above the search box labeled "Search." Otherwise, people could get confused.

● **Top right of page position**
The ideal position for the search box is the top right of the page. The search box should be available on every page.

● **Default to searching entire website**
When someone initiates a search, their expectation is that they will be searching the entire website; so that's the way it should be.

● **Avoid advanced search features**
Nobody uses advanced search. (It sounds too advanced.) Just give people a nice big search box and a nice big search button, and hide any advanced search features behind a link (which practically nobody will click on).

● **Regularly re-index website**
If you don't regularly re-index your website, then people will be searching through an old version of the content. That's because, when you search, you initially search an index not the actual website.

● **Consider synonym expansion**
Are there common synonyms (notebook, laptop, etc.) for your products or services? If so, make sure that, if someone searches for laptop, they also get content relating to notebooks.

● **Plan for American versus global English**
We're not simply talking about spelling differences here. When Americans want to go for a long break, they search for "vacations," whereas other English speakers might search for "holidays."

● **Plural and singular words**
If someone searches for "vacation," will you also bring them back pages with references to

"vacations"? This is a simple example, but it can get more complex.

● **Manage typos**
A typo is a spelling mistake that you'll know you made once it's pointed out. The way to deal with typos is always to publish what people searched for on the search results page. Place it at the top of the page in the search box so that, if required, people can quickly change their search words and initiate a new search.

● **Manage spelling mistakes**
Many people are awful spellers, so watch out for common misspellings of important carewords, brand names, etc., and try to offer some sort of "Did you mean . . .?" function, as provided by Google.

● **Laying out search results**
When it comes to laying out search results, you really don't want to be trying to re-invent the wheel and confusing people. Examine how Yahoo, Google, AOL, and MSN Search lay out their search results, and follow best practice.

"I'm not technical" is no longer an acceptable excuse for a professional marketing or communications executive.

Getting your search engine working well is by no means easy, and there's no point in hoping that the techies will sort all this out for you. You must be the champion of your customers. You must think how they think and search how they search.

This chapter has thrown a lot at you, but none of it is rocket science. In an age of increasing information overload, getting found quickly is not some luxury. It is a necessity. If you can master these search-related skills, you will have developed valuable expertise that will undoubtedly help your career.

10 CASE STUDY: 142% INCREASE IN SALES DUE TO KILLER WEB CONTENT STRATEGY

Study Group is a leading company in the international education industry. It specializes in providing a wide range of educational opportunities to individuals who want to study in English-speaking countries. About 35,000 students from 150 countries benefit from its programs every year.

Almost all of Study Group's revenues are agent-mediated. In this sense, the website is used primarily to help students to find the right agent rather than to generate direct sales.

The history of Study Group's websites reflects the history of website development. "In 1999, we had a corporate site and a site for one of our key academic products, Bellerbys College, with no clear business objectives for either," states Ricard Giner, manager of the Study Group Internet business department. "Both contained brochureware only. The contact details were basic, and there was no monitoring of traffic or contact."

Between 1999 and 2003, the number of Study Group websites and webpages grew substantially. However, the content remained brochureware. Most of it was directly translated from print, with little thought about how best to make it work online.

Towards the end of 2003, Study Group was facing a number of challenges with its websites:

- **No growth in traffic since 2002**
- **No growth in enquiries since 2002**
- **Broadly flat traffic and visitor behavior metrics**
- **Gradual decline in Google ranking for key search terms**
- **Increasing competition from other websites in the sector**

Embassy CES old home page

As can be seen from the images, the old home pages for Embassy CES and Bellerbys College (two Study Group colleges) were pretty much a copy of what you would see on the front cover of a brochure.

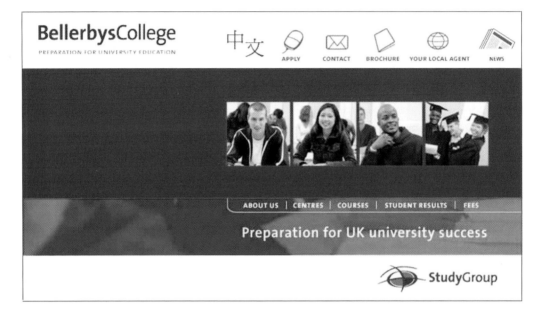

Bellerbys College old home page

Study Group had come to realize that simply placing print content on its website wasn't a viable strategy; it quite plainly wasn't delivering a return. As a result of a number of workshops, audits, and discussions, it was decided to adopt a new approach.

THE ACTIONS

Study Group used the killer Web content approach to develop a new Web strategy. This strategy needed to achieve the following key objectives.

- **Increase the number of potential students visiting its websites.**

- Increase the number of potential students returning to the website, as research indicated that the decision to take a Study Group course was made over a period of time.
- Increase the page views per visitor so that visitors would be better informed when they made an inquiry.
- Increase the quality of students' enquiries.
- Ensure that the cost of the exercise was proportional to the additional revenue generated by the websites.
- Ensure that the websites delivered a quantifiable increase in sales.

The key action points that the killer Web content approach proposed were as follows.

- Better define the target readers for each website.
- Focus on the killer content for the target readers and get rid of the filler content. (Write Web content, not print content.)
- Focus on the core tasks that readers came to the website to complete and the carewords that they pursued these tasks with.
- Improve the publishing processes. Start commissioning and scheduling content. Put proper editing and review processes in place. Motivate and reward the editors and writers.
- Create content that will improve the chances of being found in the first page of major search engines' results.
- Have an ongoing strategy to acquire new links from third parties.

The following table outlines how Study Group went about these tasks.

Requirement	Action
Define target readers	• Carried out market analysis. • Consulted with market specialists. • Asked readers (students) what they wanted. • Examined successful competitor websites.
Define killer content	• Distinguished clearly between the killer and the filler. • Structured publication plan around what students want to see and need to see, rather than what Study Group want to give them.
Focus on tasks and carewords	• Found that what students care about most is hearing the stories of other students. • Wrote for the students, rather than at them, and where possible got students to write content that recounted their experiences of studying with Study Group. • Overhauled classification entirely to create a smaller set of classifications that were careword-focused.
Improve publishing processes	• Appointed a full-time Web editor and writers who had Web writing as part of their job profile. (This addressed motivation and reward.) • Turned Web publishing into a more rigorous discipline with deadlines and a defined editing process. • Separated the print publishing process from the Web publishing process. • Rewrote all Web content, based on Web writing rules as articulated by the killer Web content approach. • Gave Web writing seminars to all those involved.
Get found in search	• Activated strategy to research and go after appropriate third party links. • Wrote page titles and other relevant metadata from the point of view of how students searched. • Made sure that navigation and all other links were coherent and consistent throughout the websites.

Here are the new home pages that were subsequently launched for Embassy CES and Bellerbys College.

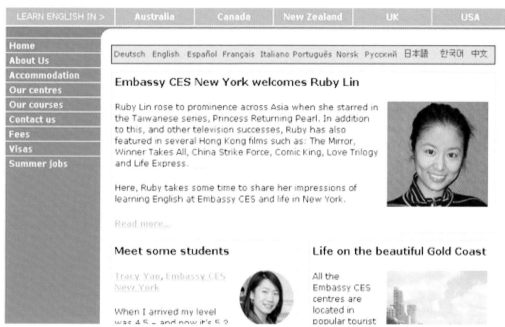

Embassy CES 2005 home page

BellerbysCollege
PREPARATION FOR UNIVERSITY EDUCATION

Apply | Contact | Brochure | Your local agent

| PREPARE FOR UNIVERSITY IN > | Brighton & Hove | Cambridge | London | Oxford |

Home
About us
Accommodation
Our centres
Our courses
Contact us
Fees
MW International Summer School
Visas
Alumni

Student results

العربية   فارسی   繁體中文   简体中文   日本語   Русский   Nigeria   English

What is home life like in the UK?

You'll find plenty of information about all our colleges on this website. But what will it be like after classes when it's time to go home?

At Bellerbys we offer two types of accommodation, residential and Homestay. You can choose whether you prefer live in student accommodation, or with a British family. In residential accommodation, you'll learn some independence, and it's good preparation for life at university. If you prefer company, and the comforts of home, then Homestay is the better option for you.

See what our students say about Bellerbys accommodation...

Meet some staff at Bellerbys

Andy Quin, Bellerbys London

See our new centre at London Greenwich

Bellerbys College 2005 home page

Study Group found that the real killer Web content was carefully crafted student stories. Potential students often found themselves in a situation where they would be leaving home for the first time for a prolonged period. In an uncertain world, they needed to know that they would fit in and that they would be comfortable and safe in their new surroundings.

Seeing the face of a student – and, better still, the face of a student of their own nationality – on the Study Group home page was a great start. However, it was much more than just a face. This wasn't the face of some nameless student that might have attended a course many years ago; it was the face of named student who was attending a Study Group course now. And they are telling it like it is, in their own words.

To create such killer Web content on a consistent basis, Study Group has started a student club initiative. According to Ricard Giner, "This will offer a rich online experience tailored to the needs of individuals wishing to study abroad, and publishing students' own perspectives on the study abroad experience, via forums, community-style Web environments, testimonials, quizzes, questionnaires, competitions, and 'rate the school'-type pages."

THE RESULTS

Embassy CES and Bellerbys were the first two Study Group websites to implement the killer Web content approach. Here are some of the measurable outcomes.

Embassy CES

1. Unique visitors up 68%

2. Visits up 172%

3. Page views up 83%

4. Returning visitors up 127%

5. Unique enquirers up 47%

6. Sales up 37%

Bellerbys College

1. Unique visitors up 84%

2. Visits up 208%

3. Page views up 129%

4. Returning visitors up 194%

5. Unique enquirers (remarkably) down 10%

6. But sales up 142%

By focusing on the killer rather than the filler content, Study Group was able to get more qualified enquiries coming through. For Bellerbys College, while the number of unique enquirers actually dropped by 10%, sales went up by 142%. Fewer tire kickers, less sales costs, more profit. That's what killer Web content is about.

The ranking of important Study Group carewords in major search engines has also improved substantially. "For key search phrases such as 'English schools in London' or 'English courses in Oxford' in the market languages that matter, such as Italian, Spanish, or Japanese, we have gone from being over 100 in the rank (i.e. ten pages in) to being in the top ten (i.e. in the first page), and, in many cases, first," Ricard Giner states.

"I think these figures speak for themselves," Mr. Giner continues. "We have carried out almost no promotion, but have rather focused almost entirely on Gerry McGovern's advice. We can safely attribute these significant improvements in our key metrics and the sales growth to the McGovern approach to Web content publication."

PART THREE:
THE BORING

(But Important) Stuff

RESEARCHING FOR THE KILLER WEB CONTENT

You need to do some research to make sure you have the right raw materials to build your killer Web content. The world is changing fast, and so you have to do ongoing research to ensure that your knowledge is up to date and to identify the new skills you will need to develop if you want your career to progress. Research keeps you sharp, keeps your knowledge relevant, and keeps you ahead.

Spending time upfront is about saving time down the line.

GO TO THE SOURCE: TALK TO PEOPLE

While there is a huge quantity of information on the Web, I'm sure you've found that some of the most valuable knowledge you've acquired has been the result of talking to people. You can't beat getting it from the source; you can't beat reading the body language.

When should you talk to people instead of just searching on the Web?

- **When you need to develop case studies or client testimonials.**
- **When you have experts within your organization who have valuable knowledge but don't have the time, inclination, and/or ability to write it down.**

- **If your subject is new: the newer the subject, the less likelihood there is that much has been published on it.**
- **If the information you seek is important: the more valuable the information you are seeking, the less likely it is that it will be on the Web, certainly in a free format.**
- **If you seek exact information: the greater the need for absolute accuracy, the better off you are checking your facts against offline sources.**

Of course, it's not always an either/or situation; usually it's a combination that works. Just remember that everyone is searching the Web. Going to the source may be what gives you the edge.

The best information can be the hardest to find. That's why it's the best.

Talking to people is not as simple as it sounds. It's not just about giving someone a call and asking a few questions. It's time-consuming and it takes a lot of experience to get it right. People will tell you one thing while their body language or tone of voice tells you something else. It takes lots of practice to get good at reading people.

A more formal approach to talking to people is to carry out an interview. If you want to become good at interviews, be prepared to do a lot of them. Below are the typical time frames involved in doing a one-hour interview.

- **It can take between one and two hours to prepare the questions. It can take much longer if you are unfamiliar with the subject, requiring you to do several hours of preliminary research. However, don't feel you have to** be an absolute expert; you need to know enough to be able to ask intelligent questions.

- It can take anywhere from ten minutes to several days to arrange the interview. This depends on how senior the person is you are trying to reach, and plain luck.
- It will take three hours or more for a full transcription – typing out exactly what was said. Then you'll need to turn the transcript into a meaningful report, which will take several more hours.

HOW TO DEVELOP YOUR INTERVIEWING SKILLS

The following guidelines will help you improve your interviewing skills.

- Good interviewers care about their subject, have a genuine interest in and desire to learn from people, and are never afraid to chase someone if they know there is something valuable to learn. They show gratitude and are polite and friendly.
- To get killer, give killer. People are much more likely to give you information if you can give them something as well. The more important the person you are trying to reach, the more important it is that you have something valuable to give them.
- If you're interviewing a number of people, start with the most junior. That way you can hone your questions and gather interesting information to pass on to the more senior people.
- Prepare. Getting the questions right and in the right order is 50% of the interview process. Never interview people without knowing as much as possible about their background.
- Be determined and develop a thick skin. Frequently, the people you really need to talk to will be the hardest to reach and will often say no initially. Learn to brush it off and to be polite and persistent – a delicate balance.

- Be a good networker. It's always easier to get people to talk to you if you can tell them someone they know said you should speak to them. Better still, get that someone to put in a good word for you.
- Never start a conversation without having a clear idea of what you want out of it.
- Ask one question at a time. The more important the person, the more valuable their knowledge, and the more questions you will want to ask. Don't fire off a barrage of questions, though, as you'll only annoy them
- Use silence. When you ask a question, wait for the answer. It's not your opinion you're looking for, it's the opinion of the person you're talking to. Most people don't like silences and will talk to fill them up.
- Be a good listener – it's harder than you think. Focus on what the person is saying. Listen carefully; don't be distracted by your next question, your next call, or your lunch meeting. If the person is worth talking to, they're worth listening to.
- Don't be afraid to ask "stupid" questions. If you've done some research and you're still not clear about something, ask. There's no point in pretending to know just so the other person won't think you're ignorant; that's a great way to remain ignorant.
- When you're interviewing someone, make sure the ground rules are clear:
  - Clarify how you will use what the person says. Specify whether you are just going to use it for yourself or if you intend to publish it in an article.
  - If you are recording the interview, explain what you will do with the tapes. State how long you will keep them and how you will dispose of them.

IMPROVING YOUR WEB SEARCHING SKILLS

A researcher once told me that, after observing numerous groups of people searching, it was clear that few wanted to learn how to search better. They just wanted results as quickly as possible. If the first page of results didn't look promising, they'd try some new carewords. If results for these still didn't look promising, most would assume that what they were looking for wasn't on the Web. Hardly anybody wanted to use advanced search, let alone an offline source.

This is an opportunity for you because, if you can learn some basic search skills and take more time when preparing your search, you will be more efficient – and ultimately faster – at finding exactly what you need.

Here are some things to keep in mind when searching on the Web.

- **Plan.** Take a few minutes to think about what it is you are searching for. Step back; don't rush in. Clarifying exactly what it is you want to find will save wading through too many irrelevant results. Spend five minutes finding out about the advanced search features of the search engine you're using.

- **Be patient and persistent.** If you're not getting the results you expect, rethink your approach. Is there another way of framing this search?

- **Be specific, then broad.** There's so much stuff out there that you need to start your search in a reasonably specific manner. Then, if you're getting too few – or the wrong type of – results, broaden out. Here are some tips:
  - **Use at least two carewords. Generally, it is not a good idea to place a single careword in the search box.**
  - **Try the obvious first. Don't try to be too clever in**

choosing your carewords. Use the ones that seem the most natural and obvious.

- Put your most important carewords first.
- Use quotation marks if you know an exact quote from what you are looking for. So "sales of product X rose 17%" is much more likely to get you the webpage that exact quote comes from than if you enter those words without the quotation marks.

● Don't rely on just one search engine. You probably have a favorite search engine, and that's okay. Just remember that even the best search engine can be weak at certain searches. You should have two to three other search engines bookmarked to try when you're not getting the results you want.

● Think like the writer. If your obvious carewords fail, try to get inside the head of the writer of the content you need. What sort of carewords would they use? How would they phrase them?

● Use a thesaurus. If your chosen carewords are not bringing back the results you require, use a thesaurus to expand your careword range.

● Consider directories. If you really don't know where to start with your search or if you have a classification in mind, such as American PR agencies, try a Web directory like Yahoo or DMOZ. These can be useful for certain types of searches.

USE INTERNET DISCUSSION FORUMS AND BLOGS

Internet discussion forums can be valuable resources for your research. These can range from web-based discussion forums to e-mail discussion lists. Here you will find people discussing a particular subject. For example, there are lots of great discussion forums on search engine optimization and marketing (High Rankings is one that I frequent: www.highrankings.com/forum).

Forums can be a good source of content but they should not be your only source, as they can be open to manipulation. People with ulterior motives may be pretending to be "normal" customers. For example, an error occurred on the Amazon.com website that exposed the personal details of "customers" writing book reviews, and it turned out that many authors were using false names to write reviews of their own books.

Blogs can be useful for research, and you should certainly be aware of any blogs where people are writing about your organization. Sure, lots of blogs out there have little value, but spend the time to research the good ones, because some of the world's smartest people and most severe critics are writing blogs these days. Then get some RSS software so that you are automatically informed of new content on your favorite blogs and other research sources.

GET YOUR RESEARCH FROM A WIDE RANGE OF SOURCES

It's not a good idea to depend on a single source for your research. One of the key skills you should develop is how to draw the balance of truth from multiple sources. There are multiple versions of any event. Some of them are downright lies, some are simply inaccurate, and others have varying levels of value. It's up to you to sort out what you need to keep and what you need to ignore, to analyze and evaluate the credibility of each source. You will be establishing your own point of view based on research from many sources; so don't talk to just one person or read just one website or book.

Trust is hard won and easily lost.

CHECK YOUR FACTS

Be careful how you use the results of your research. It's easy to get it wrong; it takes work to be accurate. Research is almost always about maximizing the input and minimizing the output. Scan-readers – the people who will be reading your writing – love facts. They're like juicy meat to a hungry dog. But the facts must be correct, or you're throwing poison to that dog.

Trust is hard won and easily lost. If you deliver inaccurate or misleading information to people, you damage your reputation.

If you're using facts in your content:

- **Print out the document and physically mark every fact that requires verifying.**
- **Be skeptical. Who said this? Are they reliable?**
- **If the name of an organization or brand is mentioned, check the relevant website to verify spelling.**
- **If possible, don't use secondary sources to confirm facts, as that secondary source may not have done its fact-checking correctly. You'd be amazed how a mistake, once it gets published, can spread like a virus. Just because the *New York Times* published it doesn't mean it's true.**
- **If you have to use secondary sources, find at least two and make sure they agree. If possible, make sure that one of them is from a recognized printed source.**
- **Check phone and fax numbers and Web and e-mail addresses. Ring them up; send an e-mail; test the website address in your browser.**
- **Don't mix up your currency symbols (dollars, pounds, euros, etc.).**

ALLOCATE SOME TIME TO BROAD RESEARCH

Allocate a little time every week – perhaps an hour – to broadening your research. Follow whatever links take your fancy and don't worry about focus; instead, go with the flow. The creative mind needs to be jolted and surprised; it needs to be presented with information it's not used to. Otherwise, it can get stuck in a rut.

Now and then, follow a link that it makes absolutely no sense to follow.

Habit is essential if you want to be effective and get things done in the most efficient manner possible. However, habit is not that great for creativity, as it results in automatic behavior.

Bringing fresh and unexpected things to the mind can help it to think the unexpected. Most mad ideas are mad, but a few of them change the world; so allow yourself a little bit of madness – it's good for you.

Even the most well-planned research can open up unexpected paths. You must be able to think on your feet. So, if it's interesting enough, follow it. A new question might come to mind during an interview. If it's interesting enough, ask it.

Remember, research is a process not a project. The world is indeed changing, and research gets you on top of things.

12 THE IMPORTANCE OF BEING ORGANIZED

What is an organization if not organized?

Imagine a modern factory floor. It is professionally designed, clean, well lit, safe, and efficient. Very little is out of place, which results in everything running smoothly. That's because we have become very good at organizing the physical world.

Now imagine the inside of your Intranet, your public website, or your computer. If you turned all your content into something physical – something you could walk through – would it look like that efficient factory floor or would it look more as if you had emptied a dustbin on the floor?

A lot of content is badly organized, which means that it's harder to find, harder to understand, and harder to put into context, and this makes it a time drain. The impatient scan-reader – Mary, Johan or Tomas – absolutely hates time drains. So you may well have killer Web content, but, because of bad organization, it gets smothered by the filler. With so much stuff out there, the ability to organize has never been more critical.

While a great many people like the idea of creating content, they don't like the boring procedure of organizing it. In popular thinking, organization and creativity are not often associated, the hallmark of creative people supposedly being that they think outside the box. (People hate to be placed in boxes unless, of course, that box happens to be a house, office, elevator, car, train, ship, or plane. And how could you move house if you had no boxes? Boxes and walls are containers; containers are a tool of organization.)

Organization does not have to be the enemy of creative thinking. Very often, the creative genius is extremely well organized. The poet, W.B. Yeats, established very sophisticated structures for his writing, as did James Joyce. J.K. Rowling planned how many *Harry Potter* books she'd write, and had written the last chapter of the last book at an early stage. J.R.R. Tolkien could not have written *The Lord of the Rings* if he hadn't been extremely well organized.

The mind "is a self-organizing system," according to Edward de Bono. "The purpose of the brain is to allow experience to organize itself into patterns – and then to use these existing patterns."

ORGANIZE FOR THE CUSTOMER

The Web challenges us all to organize around the customer, whoever that customer is. The organization that succeeds on the Web is the one that puts the customer at the very centre of everything it does. A great website lets customers quickly do the things they need to do, rather than forcing them to do things the way the organization wants them to.

When you organize your Web content, put the customer at the very centre of the structure. Find out the tasks of your customer and make them the foundation of the classification of your website. This is how you succeed on the Web. This is how you make the sale, deliver the service, and build your brand.

You are an organization of one in a network of many.

In your personal space, your desk, for example, can be a little messy if you know where you can quickly lay your hands on whatever you need. In your public space – your website, blog, or intranet – there is much less room for messiness. Collaboration, as we'll see in the next chapter, is a major trend in content creation. To collaborate, you need to share content. If, however, your content is not easy to find and is not put in a context that can be understood by your collaborators (customers), it will make it difficult to share and collaborate on.

CLASSIFICATION: IT'S A DIRTY JOB BUT SOMEONE'S GOT TO DO IT

The FirstGov home page shown overleaf is almost entirely made up of classifications and task-focused links. Classification is the ultimate distillation of what your organization does and stands for. It should be built from carewords.

Nobody likes to classify. Even in libraries – the home of classification – the job is avoided, particularly by men. I was once told a story about the difference between male and female librarians. A typical male librarian loves a challenge. Let's say you come in and ask for a book called *Fly Fishing in Longford* that was published in 1994. That's a pretty hard-to-find book, the male librarian will tell you. Nevertheless, he'll go searching, checking with other libraries and with lots of databases.

Every day, books get returned to the library and they begin to stack up. At some point, someone decides to take the stack of books and place them back on their shelves. Like magic, the male librarians disappear. They have important phone calls to make or they're trying to find a really obscure book. Female librarians don't like putting books back on shelves either, because it is boring work. They do know, however, that if you don't put the books back in their rightful places in the classification, you'll never be able to find that really obscure book on *Fly Fishing in Longford*.

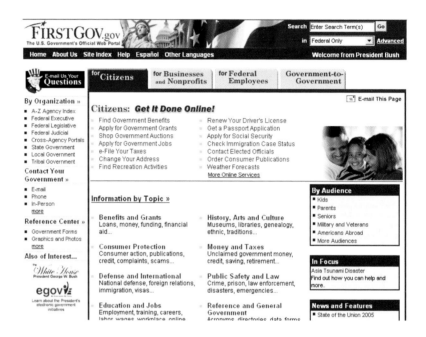

Don't expect software to do the classification work for you. Classification is essentially a human skill.

The Web has been described as a library – one with all the books on the floor and the lights turned out. Very few websites do classification well, and there are a few simple reasons for this situation:

- **Websites were usually designed by men, many of whom felt that classification was a menial task that required little effort or planning.**
- **Many of these men were techies who had an almost fanatical belief that technology would sort out every problem.**
- **Classification is, in fact, extremely difficult to get right. It requires rigor, subtlety, marketing and communication savvy, political awareness, experience, and learning.**

If you can become good at classification design, you will have acquired a key skill that will help you to make yourself invaluable in a world drowning in information overload. Good classification design requires tremendous organizational skills and is not something that can be easily outsourced or automated.

Before you write, think about how your content will be classified.

Throughout your career, you will find yourself dealing with classification. Classification is a cornerstone of all Web design. As a creator of content, you will need to identify what classification your content will be placed under. If your content is not classified well, it might as well not exist, since unclassified content is much harder to find in a sprawling sea of information. Therefore, before you write anything of substance, ask questions such as:

- **How will what I want to write be classified?**
- **Does this classification have too much content in it already?**

- **Does this classification have enough? Maybe I should create some content for it?**
- **Do I really have two ideas here, each of which fits in a distinct classification?**
- **Maybe I should write two shorter pieces of content, rather than one long one?**

HOW TO DESIGN AN EFFECTIVE CLASSIFICATION

Designing a classification is not easy, whether it is for the files on your computer or your e-mails; or a section of an intranet or a public website. It takes time and effort. It requires patience and long-term planning. There is no simple way around it, no easy solution or quick fix.

A classification is built from carewords. Chapter 6 has given you the techniques to discover your carewords. Now here are some tips, based on the "six Cs" (see Chapter 5), that will help you to design the best classification structure possible from your carewords.

GET THE TOP LEVEL DESIGNED FIRST

The top-level classification is the classification your reader will see on your home page.

It's important to spend as much time as is necessary on the top level because, if you get it right, everything else tends to fit into place. If you get it wrong, you're going to have a lot of problems.

Top-level classification is very political.

It is absolutely vital that you get your top-level classification signed off by all the key stakeholders in the project. Do not make the fatal mistake of assuming that senior managers don't care about the classifications that appear on the home page. They do care – or will care – so you must get them involved. I have seen many Web projects come to grief due to this oversight.

Make sure you visualize your classification as quickly as possible. Classification is one of the most difficult challenges you will face, and it helps if you can see the classification on a screen or a mock-up of it on a printed page, flip chart, whiteboard, etc.

MAKE IT COMPELLING AND USE CAREWORDS

Who is the classification for and what do they care about? (Is it for Mary, our devoted mother, or Tomas, our young ambitious doctor? Or is it for both of them?) Let's say you've been asked to make a classification for heart disease. If you were classifying the subject for patients and caregivers, then you would try to think like them. Ask yourself the question: What would somebody who has heart disease, who suspects they have heart disease, or who is caring for someone with heart disease want to know? How do you choose carewords that are compelling to them? You might consider using some of the following:

- **heart disease symptoms**
- **heart disease first signs**
- **women and heart disease**
- **men and heart disease**
- **heart disease prevention**
- **heart disease treatment**
- **heart disease risk factors**
- **heart disease main causes**
- **heart disease and diet**
- **reversing heart disease**
- **heart disease aftercare**

MAKE IT CLEAR

Classification is about ordering content into logical groups so it can quickly be found again. It is also about helping establish context. If someone finds a particular piece of content, they'll be able to see what related content has been classified with it. If you're classifying for doctors, then it may make sense to use "cardiovascular disease," but for the general public "heart disease" might be a better choice of words.

It's easy to get carried away with classification design and to strive to develop some sort of perfect system. That's not a good idea. Be clear and practical in your approach. Your classification needs to be used; so use the most commonly understood and shortest carewords.

MAKE IT COMPLETE

The world changes, and so to some degree you are always classifying against a moving target. The classification system you design today might not be an exact fit in 12 months, but that doesn't mean it won't still do the job just fine.

There may be new breakthroughs in heart disease medicine, but the way a patient or caregiver approaches gathering information about heart disease will probably not change all that much. Whatever the new treatment, they will still have the same basic tasks: to find out more about prevention, symptoms, first signs, treatment, and aftercare.

Make it complete, and plan how your classification will stand up over the long term. Work out the overall challenges you face with your classification. You need to design a logical task path for your classification, something that fulfils the needs of the person who will access it. For the heart disease example, there may be a logical path from symptoms to treatment to aftercare.

Design your classification based on the tasks of your customers, never on the structure of your organization. Not only is a task-focused approach more logical, it also has much greater longevity, while organization structures come and go.

While you want to be complete you must also be realistic. Where's all the killer content going to come from to fill out these classifications? Who's going to review all this content to ensure that it remains relevant? Don't build a classification that is beyond your capacity to professionally manage. Think hard about this. Over the years I have come across many organizations that created grand classification schemes that quickly fell into disrepair.

MAKE IT CONCISE

Agree on the range of classifications at any particular level. If you put too many classifications at any one level, you overload people (too many jams to choose from). If you put too few, people have to click too many times to get to the content they need. Aim for ten or fewer classifications per level.

Agree on the number of levels of classification. The more levels you have, the more complex it will be to classify content and the more difficult it will be to navigate. Aim for a three-level classification design or at maximum a five-level one.

KEEP IT CORRECT

Classification design is a process. Certainly, it's a project to design the initial classification system. However, every time you misclassify or have content you don't have a classification for, you undermine the design. Classification is a living, breathing, and ongoing process; so keep it correct.

A classification design is only as good as the people who classify the content.

As you approach classification design, keep foremost in your mind that you – and probably others – must place content in this system on an ongoing basis. If it's not designed so that it is clear and quickly understood, misclassification will result.

Avoid duplication. One of the biggest potential pitfalls in designing a classification system is to create two categories that essentially mean the same thing. This confuses everybody and should be avoided at all costs. If you're creating a tourism classification, for example, you're going to have to choose between "deals" and "special offers."

Some people are too busy to classify their content well. Don't be one of them. If you have time to write it, you must make time to classify it. Otherwise, you significantly reduce the chances of it being found. If your content isn't found, it becomes like the tree that fell in the forest and that nobody heard fall.

13 COLLABORATIVELY CREATED CONTENT ROCKS

Smart people have always collaborated. "The key to a high IQ is social harmony," Daniel Goleman writes in *Emotional Intelligence*. "Things go more smoothly for the standouts because they put time into cultivating good relationships with people whose services might be needed in a crunch as part of an instant ad hoc team to solve a problem or handle a crisis."

The main effect of globalization – of which outsourcing is a sub-trend – is to create a network, by which the world is becoming an increasingly interlinked and interdependent place. Everywhere, networks are growing: the Internet, wireless and wired communications networks, and road, air, and sea networks.

It pays to collaborate.

"The manufacture of a body is a cooperative venture of such intricacy that it is almost impossible to disentangle the contribution of one gene from another," Richard Dawkins writes in *The Selfish Gene* (Oxford University Press, 3rd ed., 2006). "Selection has favored genes that cooperate with others."

There are many reasons why it makes sense to collaborate today, particularly when it comes to creating content. There was a time, not too long ago, when an educated person could keep reasonably up to date with their specialty by their own efforts. That is simply no longer possible.

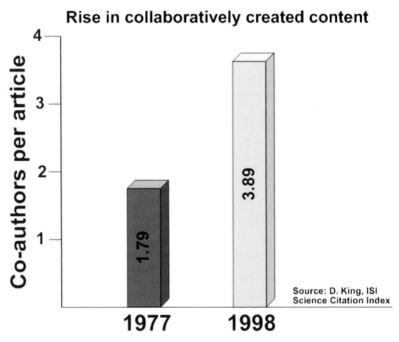

Rise in collaboratively created content

Source: D. King, ISI
Science Citation Index

I wrote earlier about the "publish or perish" rule in academia. Well, it seems like academics have discovered that they will publish far more effectively if they collaborate. In 1977, it was estimated that the average academic article written in the U.S. had 1.79 co-authors. By 1998, this had risen to 3.89. E-mail and the Web drove this substantial growth.

Basically, the historical tools of writing – the pen and paper – militated against collaboration. The tools of the network – e-mail and the Web – make collaboration more likely. As your career progresses, you will find that you will be working increasingly with other people to create content. In a fast changing world, collaboration can keep you current in a way that working on your own might not – many minds can be greater than one.

DISCOVER THE SECRET OF GENIUS

To be able to collaborate well, you must be able to give freely and – just as important – take freely. A lot of people, when they come across a great idea, won't simply accept it as a great idea and take it and use it effectively. Whether it is arrogance or an inferiority complex, or a mixture of both, some people feel that, if they don't come up with the idea themselves, or at least substantially alter it, they cannot use it.

Geniuses steal. Beggars borrow.

Contrary to popular myth, geniuses tend to be good collaborators. Stravinsky, for example, collaborated vigorously, as did Picasso. Great thinkers are always interested in great ideas, wherever they come from. They combine a child-like fascination with life with an adult discipline of getting things done. Great artists will work with others if they can see that the results will be productive.

Focus on your strengths, collaborate on your weaknesses.

One of the most important things you should do in your life is to discover the things you are not good at and stop doing them. I have come across many people who focus on their weaknesses, trying vainly to excel in an area they are not suited to. At the same time, they ignore key strengths, mistakenly thinking that what comes naturally either mustn't be of much value or doesn't need to be worked hard on to achieve true excellence.

Are you good at ideas, writing, researching, or editing? Identify your strengths and weaknesses when it comes to content, and then focus

PUT SOMEONE IN CHARGE

I wrote a book once with two other people. We had to put someone in charge who would set and police deadlines and implement edits to the text. I don't like having someone in charge – unless that person happens to be me. The only thing I like less than having someone in charge other than me is having nobody in charge.

If you are in charge, keep in mind this quote from Warren Bennis in *Organizing Genius*: "Great groups are inevitably forged by people unafraid of hiring people better than themselves." Great collaborators know what they don't know and know what they're not good at.

Don't micromanage. Apple, Disney, Lockheed Martin Skunk Works, and the Manhattan Project were all places where great collaboration occurred. Many of these collaborative efforts had difficult leaders; however, one thing that most of them didn't do was micromanage. They tended to select great people and let them at it. If any of them didn't meet the standards expected, then they got bawled out of it, of course.

A FINAL WORD

(883, to be exact)

14 YOUR WORDS ARE POWERFUL THINGS

"Whatever words we utter should be chosen with care, for people will hear them and be influenced by them for good or ill."
– Buddha

"Without knowing the force of words, it is impossible to know men."
– Confucius

"Words are, of course, the most powerful drug used by mankind."
– Rudyard Kipling

"Give me 26 lead soldiers and I will conquer the world."
– Benjamin Franklin

"Be careful about reading health books. You may die of a misprint."
– Mark Twain

If you have a flair for content, this is your time. The world's economy might run on oil, but it also runs on content. If you stopped the flow of oil, you would cause serious problems. What would happen if the Internet and all the other content networks were shut down? Content matters; it's just that it hasn't received the attention it deserves yet.

Developing the skills of a Web editor gives you a really bright future. Like all editors, you will focus first and foremost on knowing your reader. It's funny, but in this age of computer technology, management will become less about managing technology and more about managing people and understanding emotions. You will learn to understand what your reader really cares about – the killer Web content.

Writing quality content is very demanding work, according to a series of tests completed by Ronald T. Kellogg and reported in his book *The Psychology of Writing*. Participants in the tests were asked to carry out a number of tasks: learning, reading, novice chess, expert chess, and writing. A bell would go off at random intervals during these tests, with participants being measured on how fast they responded to hearing the bell. Basically, the more concentration the task required, the slower their response would be. (Their responses were measured in milliseconds (ms).)

Learning and reading activities took about 200 milliseconds in response time, while novice chess took about 300. The expert chess players took about 400 milliseconds to respond, while those engaged in writing took just a little less time to respond (around 380 milliseconds). So, based on Kellogg's research, writing is just a little easier in mental effort than playing expert chess.

It requires a lot of mental effort to create killer Web content, but that's a good thing. If it was easy, it would quickly be automated or outsourced – or else everyone would be doing it. This is an age that rewards quality content like no other. Whether you are blogging, writing e-mails, or creating content for your intranet or public website, your words can have real potency. Properly crafted, they can help your organization to achieve its objectives more effectively, and, in so doing, further your career.

It is perfectly okay to be apprehensive about writing; it is a difficult task and many professional writers have felt apprehensive. Being hard on your writing gives you a critical objectivity that will help you to produce a better result. (Those who think their writing is utterly brilliant often end up writing vain, empty words.) You are not alone if you stare at a blank page, wondering how you are going to get started; that fear is as old as writing itself.

This may be an age of convenience foods and instant gratification, but some things still take time to acquire, and the ability to write well is one of them. You *can* learn to create killer Web content, but it will take time and effort. And that should be a positive from your point of view, because many other people will be too "busy" to put in the time and effort, giving you the edge.

To create killer Web content, you must maximize the input and minimize the output. Your effort to create this content will be like a marathon, but the content itself will be like a sprint: short and punchy. To get on the track of creating killer Web content, you should therefore establish a schedule for your writing.

Some of the most productive and talented writers have followed a regular writing schedule and have even established rituals. (Ernest Hemingway supposedly sharpened 20 pencils before writing, and W. Somerset Maugham wrote until precisely 12.45 p.m. every day.) Research indicates that the typical behavior of a writer is to write in the morning, and then to revise, research, and plan in the afternoon. Find the schedule that works best for you and then stick to it. Good writing is achieved as a result of a long-term process not a once-off project.

"We all have heard that the average online conversion rate tops out at about 2%," Bryan Eisenberg, founder of Future Now, Inc., writes. "What you probably don't know is that the average offline catalogue retailer that moves online has an average conversion rate of 6%. That's three times better than average! Why? Their words."

Offline catalogue retailers know the value of content. They know that words can make the sale, deliver the service, and build the brand. For most organizations, Web content is still a hidden asset, and they are accidental publishers. Focus on your readers, their tasks, and their carewords, and you will tap this asset and reap rich rewards.

APPENDIX 1: Great Irish Holidays carewords list

32 counties
360° Dublin
about Ireland
about us
accommodation
activities
advertise
air travel
arts and culture
arts enthusiast
attractions
basics
best of Ireland
book travel
books
books and talks
bookstores
car rental
cars/rail
children
cinema
clubbing
comedy
community
contact us
contests
conventions
cruises
cultural tips
culture
currency converter
customer service
canoe
meals
destinations
dining
Dublin
e-cards
environment
cents
exhibitions
explore the region
facts for the traveler
feedback
flights
food and drink
further reading
gardens
genealogy

general tips
getting here and around
gigs
guides and advice
health and safety
history
history buff
home
hotels
Irish vacation packages
journals
leisure
literature
live views
maps
message boards
Midlands East
money and costs
museums
music
must-see activities
nature
news
newsletters
nightlife
Northern Ireland
Northwest
off the beaten track
outdoor activities
packages and cruises
packing list
places to visit
planning a trip
pubs
pubs and restaurants
queer Dublin
rain lover
regions
restaurants
school visits
Shannon
shop-a-holic
shopping
sights and activities
Southeast
Southwest
souvenirs
spa and sports nut
special offers

sports and activities
stage
sun worshipper
the best active vacations
the best bird-watching
the best castles
the best family attractions
the best gardens
the best golf courses
the best literary spots
the best luxury hotels
the best moderately priced hotels
the best natural attractions
the best of ancient Ireland
the best picture-postcard
   small towns
the best pubs
the best ruins
the best restaurants
theatre
things to do and see
tips and resources
top sights
tourist advice
tourist information centers
tourist traps
tours
trail blazer
transport
travel bookings
travel insurance
travel talk
urban explorer
useful links
vacation ideas
vacations
virtual tours
warnings or dangers
weather
weekend breaks
West
what to see and do
what's coming
what's new
what's on
when to go
when to leave
winter warrior
working in tourism

Appendix 2: Government carewords list

accessibility
archive
benefits to customer
best practice
better classification
better quality metadata
bobby compliance
branding
business case
business process transformation
central/local government
centralization
centralization first steps
centralized approach success
  stories
channel strategy
citizen-focused
citizens more informed
classification
commissioning
common look and feel
community engagement
consistency
consistent navigation
content approval
content is critical
content management systems
content migration
cross-department collaboration
customer satisfaction
data protection
defining roles and responsibilities
department vs. citizen view
depth of classification
design scalability/flexibility
destination site
devolved publishing
digital divide (in society)
Disability Discrimination Act
distributed ownership
distributed publishing
document management
document repository
drawbacks of centralization
Dublin core
dynamic websites
easier to use
e-democracy
editing
e-GIF

eliminating duplication
evaluation
fast in, fast out
finding content faster
Freedom of Information Act
funding
governance
government website
  success stories
graphic design
identifying value
inaccurate content
inclusiveness
information architecture
information management
information overload
international government
website best practice
interoperability
IPSV (integrated public
  sector vocabulary)
IT department doesn't get it
just say No
keep it simple
knowing target audiences
knowledge management
lack of clear policies and
  procedures
lack of good quality
statistical information
lack of real authority
lack of resources
less is more approach
maintaining credibility of
  government content
marketing the website
metadata
metrics
MIS/performance metrics
modernizing government
more accurate search
more applications
more budget
more content
more responsive government
more staff
multi-channel delivery
multiple ways in
no clear strategy
not enough applications

not enough content
open source
out-of-date content
ownership
performance improvement
performance measures
personalization
plain language
portal
procedural/legislative barriers
procurement
promoting government
promotion of website
proving website's worth
publishing policies
putting citizens first
quality control
quality search
raising citizen awareness
realizing cost savings
reducing cost of government
releases/release strategy
repository
return on investment
RSS
saving citizens time
search engine optimization
security
semantic Web
senior management buy-in
separating content from
  infrastructure
service standards
services-oriented
architectures
serving citizens
silo mentality
simpler applications
simpler navigation
stakeholder management
style guide
support mission statement
technical capacity
testing
tone of voice
too complicated
too confusing
too many clicks
too many websites
too much to do, too little time

too slow
training
transactional services
transactions
usability

usage patterns
user feedback
visitor-friendly
Web metrics
Web review committee

website getting too big
website policies
workflow
writing for the Web
XML

Appendix 3: University carewords list

ability to explore ideas with
  lecturers
ability to switch degrees
academic departments
accessibility
accommodation
affordable accommodation
alumni
applying for grants
archive
authentication
better classification
better editing
better quality metadata
better search
branding
business case
career advice
centralization
centralization first steps
centralized approach success
  stories
city profile
classification
collaboration
commissioning
common look-and-fee
confusing navigation
consistency
consistent navigation
content is critical
content management systems
continuing education
corporate and business
  partnerships
cost of living
course materials
cross-department collaboration
current students
cutting-edge research
data protection
defining roles and responsibilities

department A-Z
departmental view vs. student
  view
departments refuse to listen
design
design scalability/flexibility
devolved publishing
distance learning
distributed publishing
drawbacks of centralization
easier to use
eliminating duplication
faculties
fees
focus on development
  of full individual
foreign students
friendly atmosphere
funding
future job prospects
getting visa for university
good canteen
good, cheap transport
governance
grant qualification criteria
grants
hard to find what you need
help with visa application
hospitality and conferencing
inclusiveness
information overload
lack of clear policies and
  procedures
lack of real authority
lecturer accessibility
less is more approach
making friends
making students feel more
  informed
metadata
metrics
more applications

more budget
too complicated
more fun
more funding
more openness
more staff
nightlife
no clear strategy
nobody in charge
not being found in search
  engines
open days
out-of-date content
overseas students
personalization
plain language
postgraduate
preparing for university
prestigious, well-recognized
  degree
promotion of website
prospective students
prospectus
proving website's worth
public events
publishing policies
putting students first
quality content
quality facilities
quality search
raising website awareness
realizing cost savings
return on investment
RSS
search engine optimization
security
senior management buy-in
short courses
silo mentality
simpler applications
simpler navigation
site security

APPENDICES

SMS notification for important news
social life
societies and clubs
sports and recreation
stakeholder management
strategy
student loneliness
student-focused
style guide
support mission
technical capacity

testing
too confusing
too many clicks
too many websites
too much to do, too little time
too slow
top quality professors/lecturers
top-ranking course
top-ranking university
training
undergraduate

university as single brand
usability
usage patterns
visa requirements
visitor-friendly
Web metrics
Web review committee
website getting too big
website policies
work experience
world class research
writing for the Web

INDEX